MARIE CACHET

The Secret of The She-Bear

An unexpected key to understand European
mythologies, traditions and tales.

Preface by Varg Vikernes

Contact : *marie.cachet@gmail.com*
YouTube : *Marie Cachet*

To my distant ancestors,
and to my children.
To the love of Truth.

Marie Cachet

PREFACE
by
Varg Vikernes

The modern man moves through time and space without knowing neither from whence he comes nor whither he goes. He has no direction. He is lost. He is like an arrow shot randomly out into the thin air : Sans purpose. Whether or not he hits something is pure chance. Who shot the arrow ? From where did he shoot it ? At what was the arrow shot ? Why did he shoot it ?

The modern man crossed the river of forgetfulness a long time ago, some time in the Stone Age, but the lost memories are still there, in his seemingly incomprehensible and certainly strange myths and fairy tales, songs and art, traditions and customs. He still lives with what he had ages ago, but has lost his ability to see even what is plain before his eyes, so he does not understand it.

Marie Cachet has with autistic precision dug deep into the past, using intuition as well as sense perception, and present to us what she has found in this book. She explains every branch on the tree, every twig and leaf, every fruit and flower, by showing us the way down the stem to the roots, and then further into the deep earth and the darkness of pre-history – where our origins lie.

This book is a key to the past and a lantern banishing the darkness of pre-history. It will enable you to understand every single ancient myth, fairy tale, traditional song, high festival, custom and all ancient art. You will be able to illuminate even the darkest chambers of the past, and understand what you see. Perhaps also, you will understand from whence you come, and where you should aim your arrow. You will know yourself, for the first time in thousands of years.

Varg Vikernes

INTRODUCTION

In Europe, we still follow many traditions with a very old origin. So old that we no longer know where they come from. Concerning some of them, we have an idea, but we're never certain.

Throughout my life, I gradually understood the links between our traditions, I understood their origin, and I realized how old they in fact were and how important they were for our ancestors and for ourselves today. I also understood that these traditions were not superstitious as often reported, but were the result of deep, ancient and complex science. In this science, which comes from the Stone Age, our ancestors the Neanderthals explained the world and its functioning with intriguing details, and it unveiled the reincarnation mechanism that managed the life of our ancestors.

In this book, I will give you the keys to understand absolutely all our traditions and our whole mythology from the complex Egyptian theogony to the phantasmagoric dwarfs, elves and ogres of the European forests, through the painted caves, the legend of King Arthur, our classic tales, our ancient and recent mortuary traditions. I'll explain you what are the dolmens, the menhirs, why we celebrate Halloween, Christmas, Easter or other festivals and the meaning of their symbols.

You will understand what are the dragons, why they have treasures, why princesses are locked in towers, and why the kings have crowns, you will understand the myth of Atlantis and the Flood, and why magicians have hats. You will understand more archaeological traditions and rituals like the worship of Mithra, and more distant traditions like the child goddess Kumari in Nepal.

In this book I will go back to the prehistoric origins of these traditions because they are what will give you the logical link between them. They are the roots that will enable you to understand them. These origins are closely connected to what is called in archaeology "the cult of the bear", whose beginnings are evident among our ancestors the Neanderthals.

All our European traditions are related, near or far to that *bear cult*. This ancestral cult itself is identical to what is more commonly called the *cult of ancestors*, and it is directly connected to what is now called "the belief in reincarnation".

At the time when studies show that certain memories can be stored in our genes (see Brian G Dias J & Kerry Ressler: *Parental olfactory experience influences behavior and neural structure in subsequent generations*, December 2013), I wish, in this introduction, to define the concept of reincarnation.

Reincarnation, metempsychosis (Ancient Greek μετεμψύχωσις / metempsúkhôsis: *movement of the soul*) or palingenesis (from παλινγενεσία / *palingenesia*: παλίν / *palin: again*, and γένεσις / *genesis: birth*) refers to the phenomenon by which "the soul" after physical death is incarnated again in another human body.

This definition is very simple, yet it contains immense complexity. Indeed, it assumes that there is a soul. And even if we call "the personal identity" the soul, how then can it be completely differentiated from the body? Is my body not a part of my identity?

But above all, how will I find myself in another life when my genes will obviously differ? Are my genes not my brain and my brain my genes?

When I was little, I wondered a lot about people's identity. I wondered why I could control myself, but not others. And then I left aside these questions. Today, I found them again. Yes, why are you *you* and not *me*? And why am I *me* and not *you*? We must answer these questions to understand the phenomenon of reincarnation.

1. Time and movement

For that, you also need to watch them in another way, from another angle. Through time. You know that when you inflect (a verb), there are several times: past times, present times and future times. There are generally three times. This is so often stated that it is a fully admitted fact, yet it is very simple, thanks to logic, to realize that it is wrong. There is only the present, or more precisely *the moment,* an infinitesimal moment, in fact so small that we couldn't measure it. This so small moment is nothing but the great Eternity. Eternity does not move, time does not move, the only thing that moves is... us probably. You have to see this as a geographical shift: if you think about a place, that place, at least if we can simplify, is not moving.

This place can be as huge as the universe, and with your human eyes, you can not see it all, unless you move. If you move, the world around you will seem to move. Similarly if your eyes could see the infinitude, it would be like a trip for your vision through space. It is a fact: you can not see, conceive, understand or feel all at once and all together, or the scene around you will move as you move.

Here we don't speak about the geographical dimension, but about the dimension of time. You move incessantly and always because you *live* incessantly and always. You grow, you exist, you are living: you are somehow in a vehicle for what we commonly call the future.

It's your body. Your body is moving, your DNA is traveling, visiting Eternity.

Anything that moves around you is just a Whole that does not move as you see, it is only a moment, an instant, single and total, whole; it is you who move, it is you who grow up, it is you who live, not the time. And yet, if you stop, you'll actually see even less: as a vehicle stops, the landscape will stop and you will distinguish the nuances but you will never see further than below the horizon of your sight. In fact, you will no longer see anything because the view itself, as mentioned above is already a vehicle for traveling.

Why travel? That may be the question that you ask now. Like you, I can't answer, at least not here, not now. There is already too much to do with these other issues.

We are here: an Eternity, that is to say, what we perceive as instant(s), and a vehicle: the body or DNA, which allows us to visit, entirely or not and at a given speed, probably ideal compared to some known or unknown factors. We don't know much more except that we don't disappear: what we call "death" just makes us both blind and invisible. As if we were outside a car on a fast track: we could not go far compared to other individuals in their vehicles, and we would quickly be invisible to them. At least if we see it this way: the little time we would have been visible to them during the entire duration of their trip.

The vision of a person on the side of the road will not last long, but it can however mark the memory... It might even be possible that someone drives back to pick you up. Especially if we admit that it is very important to get to *where we go*. But who would pick you up? Your relatives ? Your parents ? Your children? Or... yourself?

And what if it was you? For whom do you have the most empathy, if not by definition yourself? Will you not stop? Just think, when I wrote about *you*, stopped on the roadside, I am sure you hoped that someone would *put himself in your place.*

Remember this, and now let us write about another topic.

2. Amnesia

When a person suffers an accident, sometimes he loses his memory. Partially or completely. Sometimes the individual does not even know how to talk or to walk, he is like a newborn, he must re-learn, and often, it returns pretty fast, because in fact all or most of his memories are present, they're just shaken and disturbed.

If we take the example of a library, we get the following picture: your brain is this library and all your memories are stored in it as books. As and when you are living and learning, you acquire new books and store them carefully, to consult them as necessary. We are more or less orderly and indeed, we will have a more or less good memory. If one day you are the victim of a head injury, for example, it is possible that this library is shaken, the books fall and the shelves are left empty. In this case you will no longer function normally, even if your memories are in good condition in your brain. In the worst cases you'll not even be able to walk or talk.

This is exactly what happens with many amnesic subjects, following an accident for example. These people are not lost and there are protocols in specialized hospitals to help them recover their memory: that is to say, in our image, to store their books in the right place in order to function normally again.

When I knew that my interest in these protocols developed. These protocols are very interesting for our understanding of the world and traditions of our ancestors. Suppose the person in our example is a man who used to draw. Suppose he suffered a car accident and that his memory loss is total: he does not know how to walk, draw, write or speak properly. He does not recognize his family members anymore. The professionals will examine the profile of that person, and ask relatives to understand his personality.

They will detect that he had an interest and an aptitude for drawing, for example - but it can be anything, it can be sports, music or trivial activity of daily life - and had the habit of drinking coffee at 10 am, and maybe he liked to lie in a special position to read.

Maybe he loved practicing archery also. Health professionals will therefore use these peculiarities to recall memories in him.

Indeed, these emotional memories are more deeply embedded in him. Emotions are precisely used to print and engrave special things in us. The traditions also. You will remember more easily from a Yule/Christmas night with majestic candles and decorations, but also with specific odor, than a bland and uninteresting Yule/Christmas without colors. The more senses are stimulated, the more the emotion is stronger and the more the event is repeated, the more heavily it is printed in us.

Compared to our library, we could image it this way: Your memories and classical learning are simply stored books. Your memories about emotional or passionate learning is, meanwhile, not only stored, but their place is registered in permanent marker on the library itself, and perhaps, who knows, you have stored all your other books based on those above (by size or alphabetically after the one about drawing or archery).

But back to our amnesic man. Professionals from the hospital where he is admitted will therefore propose to him one of his drawing tools, and make him repeat the gesture, hoping that his memory will come back to him. They will show him his bow, and will make him touch it, make him feel it. They will prepare, at 10 o'clock precisely, a cup of coffee and offer it to him in his usual cup. All this to make him remember his emotional memories, and so the others that will flow from them. And the man will remember. He will remember how he drew, maybe just through the feel of paper under his pencil, which will create in him first a kind of déjà vu, and strangely he will then know how to do, and then the next day in the same exercise, he will remember *this specific drawing*, and where he then was, and with whom.

Seeing his coffee he will remember the sunlight at that time, and his apartment or office, his neighbors or coworkers. Pulling the bowstring he will remember his father, who had shown him how to do, and little by little he will recover his memories and store them properly in the library of his brain, and finally, he will become himself again.

3. The science of patterns

Like me, you know Easter. Maybe you think it is a Christian festival. In fact, as many popular sources and traditions attest, it is much older. As Christians would say, initially, this festival is "Pagan". Christian meaning is, as often, related to the meaning of the Pagan one. Of course, you know the Easter eggs. They are different from one country to another, but the tradition still remains much the same: everywhere we decorate eggs, everywhere we offer eggs, and everywhere we eat eggs. Easter eggs are still today a living tradition among European. We eat eggs, and cakes with many eggs.

Understand that by eating, you ingest; *what we eat enters our body and becomes part of our body*. To eat is that and in fact, we had better pay attention to what we eat, but that's another story... We can just go back to basics. To eat is to ingest, to let it enter into the body, and we become what we eat.

Well, there's something else. Easter occur in March or April, usually late March or early April. That is about nine months before Yule/Christmas. Nine. As human pregnancy. For now, You must believe me, and then I'll explain why little by little why I say and write here is fundamentally logical. Easter is the time when young children (about 7 years old) will recognize him as himself, as the ancestor. That is why among Christians it is the so-called resurrection of Christ.

The child will ingest real food (at seven years old, anthropologically, the child is weaned, and above all, he starts to get his adult teeth). He will ingest some external DNA, the DNA from plants or old animals, already "recycled" so to speak. Recycled especially because they come from the soil where ancestors were buried or because they come from water that flowed or in which have flowed our dead ancestors or also from the birds that have eaten the dead ancestors. Since birds are important, the eggs are important.

But that's not all. Most eggs are placed in nests in trees. The tree is a picture of the placenta in the womb. The placenta, the "blood cake" is clearly very like to a tree on the fetal face.

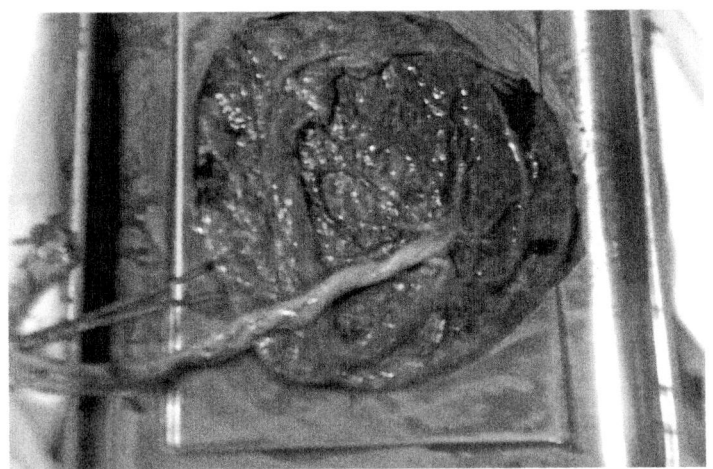

A human placenta

The blood vessels of the placenta adopt the same shape as the trunk (the umbilical cord) and branches (branched blood vessels).

Nature has designs of her own, and probably the science of our ancestors was a "science of patterns". They watched and, thanks the motives, understood the purpose and use of each thing. Sometimes they also understood as well as our modern science, and with our microscopes and our complicated tools we in fact found already understood knowledge that sometimes they actually had understood better. It is because of this science of patterns, and from this point of view on the world, that there exist now in oral and written tradition strong analogies between the "things of the world" of the same shape or design.

Today our functioning as a natural observer is subjected to the so-called modern science, who wants to have formulas and laboratory observations. Because of this conditioning we no longer understand, through the eyes and senses, the forces that govern the world and the keys left by our ancestors in our stories, traditions and mythologies.

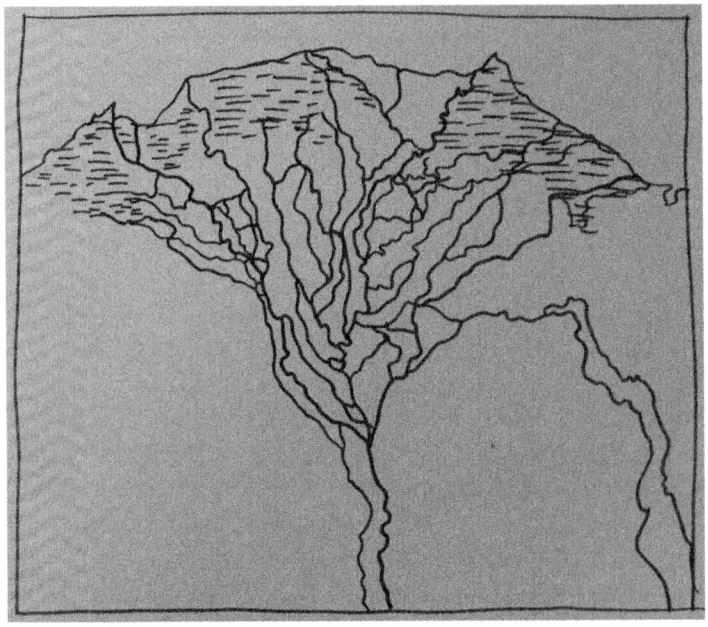

Ramifications of the Nile River

So back to the tree and the placenta...
Both are constructed on the "branches" or "ramifications" design or pattern and they interact with the element on which these branches reach.

The reason why the tree is branched is not only that it is a skeleton for a multitude of small solar panels, so to speak. *The branching pattern* governs the distribution of a fluid or a fluid exchange. Seen from the sky, streams, rivers and other rivers form a branching pattern; blood vessels form a branching pattern. The first purpose of this pattern in the tree is probably evapotranspiration.

The tree is like a water pump that supplies the liquid from the soil up to the leaves, so they can transpires it in the air.

The leaves of the tree have absolutely need for this water to avoid drying out under the effect of sunlight, they also absorb light (so it is in a way an exchange of "fluids").

The tree is interacting with the atmosphere and the universe, but also with the soil by the ramifications of the roots. The umbilical cord and ramifications or branching of the placenta, as well as blood circulation, also act as fluid exchange and interact with the placenta (or the mother) and the fetus. They pump in the clean blood and return the "dirty" blood.

You will understand soon enough that this science of patterns also provides an analogy between the mother and the atmosphere, the universe.

This tree-placenta produces fruits like the tree: the blood, the fruits of blood: red or golden apples or originally pomegranates (red for blood, golden for light). There are not just fruits, there are also eggs, placed in a nest in the tree. All this is very strongly linked and I have to explain another process before returning to these images later.

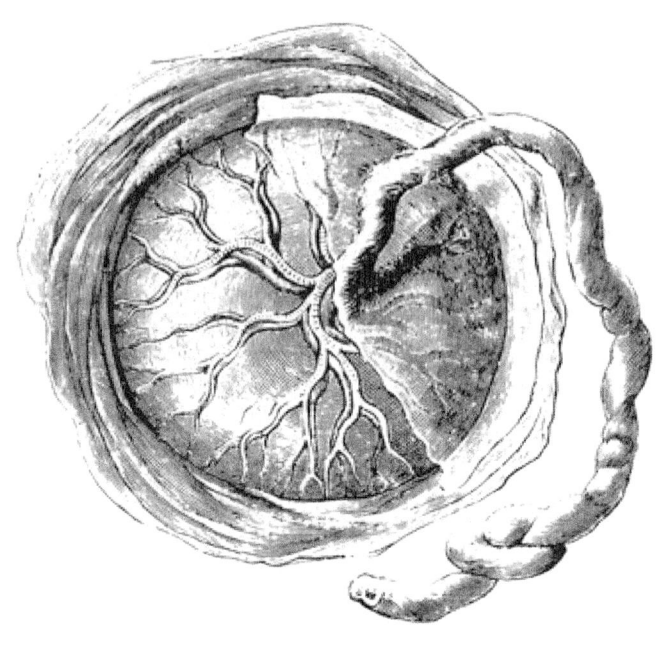

Placenta, cord and amniotic bag, fetal side

4. Crystallization

"In the salt mines, nearing the end of the winter season, the miners will throw a leafless wintry bough into one of the abandoned workings. Two or three months later, through the effects of the waters saturated with salt which soak the bough and then let it dry as they recede, the miners find it covered with a shining deposit of crystals. The tiniest twigs no bigger than a tom-tit's claw are encrusted with an infinity of little crystals scintillating and dazzling. The original little bough is no longer recognizable; it has become a child's plaything very pretty to see. When the sun is shining and the air is perfectly dry the miners of Hallein seize the opportunity of offering these diamond-studded boughs to travellers preparing to go down to the mine." (...) "I call "crystallization" that action of the mind that discovers fresh perfections in its beloved at every turn of events."
Stendhal, De l'Amour (On Love), 1822.

I will use the term "crystallization" from Stendhal to talk about a phenomenon in childhood.

How not to notice the admiring astonishment of a child for one or more heroes? It is almost a constant. When they are very small, an unrealistic hero (cartoon hero with exacerbated magic powers) is enough for them, but when they grow they need more realism, sometimes to become a "fan" of a real person. This is a kind of crystallization. The child crystallizes an ideal around a name and some facts.

The child is not actually a "fan" of the person he admires and does not know, but he is a "fan" of the ideal he created around this person. This is actually a fairly instructive phenomenon, positive and constructive.

What interests us is not this time (see *Le besoin d'impossible* written in 2009 and published in 2016) to "philosophize" on the issue of ideal, projection and crystallization, but to understand the instinctive side of this projection .

Why has the child such an instinct? The instincts are usually absolutely essential components to the species that possesses them. The baby wolf has the hunting instinct, the foal the instinct to run and escape, then why has the human child among others *the instinct of crystallization*?

Instincts are all animal or human behavior, characteristic of a species, genetically transmitted and that are expressed without any learning. These are innate impulses, automatic and invariable, that govern the behavior of all individuals of the same species.

What is the instinct of crystallization and what is seeking the human child through this crystallization around a great person?

What if this child was our man with amnesia?

What if the child remembered a part of himself in a previous life, or an ideal? What if that disposition to crystallize, at least instinctively is a disposition to go into the past, to history, to the heroes?

We know that ravens also have a family history, a learning from generation to generation, so why, in a species like ours when the learning is so important, the instinct will not turn the child to it?

Undoubtedly, our ancestors believed in reincarnation, a form of return of the soul in the flesh. Whether it was reincarnation or palingenesis (the dead feeds the soil, which feeds the plants that feeds the animals, that feeds the human beings, etc. So what is alive remains alive and becomes alive again).

This problem about reincarnation is difficult to solve. And yet. In France, we say that all the French people are the descendants of Charlemagne. In fact, not only of Charlemagne, but of all human beings of that time. Now, with DNA, we know that we are part of Charlemagne, and all human beings of that time. Really. We are even identical to a part of the tree before you. So somehow, we share something with it. Today, researchers are questioning the DNA memory, and the issued conclusions are amazing.
It is a generational memory. Some have already worked before on the question of memory. Is memory a part of our brain, or is our brain a gateway to the memory, a decryption software? Where is memory? Is there a universal memory, or at least a shared memory? It is indeed a philosophical question. But back to Charlemagne. If all the French persons are Charlemagne, then who is Charlemagne? Is it an individuality, a personality? Palingenesis does not necessarily require an individuality. Yet, archaeological discoveries and traditions suggest that our ancestors, the oldest, Neanderthals, believed that.

I want to submit a hypothesis. We know that recessive and dominant genes can be found in our DNA and, in some way, through sexual attraction, it is a form of attraction of genes for an evolutionary progress dependent of the living environment. Let us imagine that there are genes for memories. Perhaps the genes memories are attracting themselves. Maybe there are "carried" genes and actual or effective genes. Perhaps we need to have two identical copies of the same memories gene for it to be effective. Maybe *identity* is when we have sufficient amounts of effective memories genes. Maybe these copies of memory genes brought by different people throughout history (possibly recessive), are attracted to become dominant and effective.

Who knows ? Thus the individuality of the man buried there 5,000 years ago could come here now, because his memory genes scattered across his descendants returned, through sexual or loving attraction, in *one person*. Perhaps not all his memories genes, but *a sufficient amount*. As in the man with amnesia.

This would explain many things.

So I let you imagine. What if you were an important person, and if you believe in reincarnation of yourself in the future? Reincarnation in some way or another. Maybe you would be buried in a special way, you would leave traces of your passage. Maybe you would be able to find yourself? Maybe you would want to leave a legacy? Whether material or intellectual.

This is apparently what our ancestors did. Yet if you were known, it is to expect that several people in the future will mean they are yourself. Then you will maybe leave a password. This password, the secret name, it is all over in our traditions. In fairy tales, in myths...

In Egyptian mythology, Isis steals the secret name of Re to get his powers (she becomes him).

This myth is reported on *The magical Papyrus of Turin*, translated by Robert K. Ritner in 1993:

The legend of Isis and the name of Re

(...)
Now, Re entered every day in front of the crew (of the solar bark), being established on the throne of the two horizons. **A divine old age had weakened his mouth so that he cast his spittle to the earth. He spat out, it lying fallen upon the ground.** *Isis kneaded it for herself with her hand, together with the earth that was on it.*

She formed it into a noble serpent; she made (it) in the form of a sharp point. *It could not move, though it lived before her. She left it at the crossroads by which the great god passed in accordance with his heart's desire through his Two Lands.*

The noble god appeared outside, with the gods from the palace in his following, so that he might stroll just like everyday. **The noble serpent bit him, with aliving fire coming forth from his ownself.** *It raged among the pines. The divine god worked his mouth; the voice of his majesty reached up to heaven.*

(...)

"*I am a noble, son of a noble, the fluid of a god come forth from a god. I am a great one, son of a great one.* **My father thought out my name. I am one who has numerous names and numerous forms. My form exists as every god. I am called Atum and Horus of Praise. My father and mother told me my name. I have hidden it in my body from my children so as to prevent the power of a male or female magician from coming into existence against me. I went outside to see what I had made, to stroll in the Two Lands that I created, and something stung me. I do not know it. It is not really fire; it is not really water, though my heart is on fire and my body is trembling, all my members giving birth to a chill.**"

(...)

She said: "What is it, what is it, my divine father? What, a serpent has inflicted weakness upon you? One of your children has raised his head against you? Then I shall overthrow it by efficacious magic, causing him to retreat at the sight of your rays."

The holy god opened his mouth: "It was the case that I was going on the road, strolling in the Two Lands and the deserts. My heart desired to see what I had created. I was bitten by a serpent without seeing it. It is not really fire; it is not really water, though I am colder than water and hotter than fire, my entire body with sweat. I am trembling, my eye unstable; I cannot see. Heaven beats down rain upon my face in the time of summer!"

Then said Isis to Re: "Say to me your name, my divine father, for a man lives when one recites in his name."

(Re said:) "I am the one who made heaven and earth, who knit together the mountains, who created that which exists upon it. I am the one who made the water, so that the Great Swimming One came into being. I made the bull for the cow, so that sexual pleasure came into being. I am the one who made heaven and the mysteries of the horizons; I placed the ba-spirits of the gods inside it. I am the one who opens his two eyes so that brightness comes into being, who closes his two eyes so that darkness comes into being, according to whose command the inundation surges, whose name the gods do not know. I am the one who made the hours so that the days came into being. I am the one who divided the year, who created the river. I am the one who made living fire, in order to create the craft of the palace. I am Khepri in the morning, Re at noon, and Atum who is in the evening."

The poison was not repelled in its course; the great god was not comforted.

Then Isis said to Re: "Your name is not really among those that you have said to me. Say it to me so that the poison might go out, for a man lives when one pronounces his name."

The poison burned with a burning; it was more powerful than flame or fire.
Then the majesty of Re said: "May you give to me your two ears, my daughter Isis, so that my name might go forth from my body to your body. The most divine one among the gods had hidden it, so that my status might be broadened within the Bark of Millions. If there occurs a similar occasion when a heart goes out to you, say it to your son Horus after you have bound him by a divine oath, placing god in his eyes." The great god announced his name to Isis, the Great One of Magic.

"Flow out, scorpions! Come forth from Re, Eye of Horus! Come forth from the god, flame of the mouth. I am the one who made you; I am the one who sent you. Come out upon the ground, powerful poison! Behold, the great god has announced his name. Re lives; the poison is dead. The poison is dead, through the speech of Isis the Great, the Mistress of the Gods, who knows Re by his own name.

The name is in the blood: DNA, it passes "from his body to her body".

It is clear that Ra is dying, and that, to live again, the new body must know his secret name. It is by that name, and only by that name that man lives.

I give some examples here, but you will see that almost everywhere in the important ancient tales.

Homer, Odyssey, XI:

"The first that I saw was high-born Tyro, daughter of great Salmoneos (Salmoneus) and wife of Kretheus (Cretheus) son of Aiolos (Aeolus)--such was her twofold boast. She fell in love with the river-god Enipeos (Enipeus), whose waters are the most beautiful of any that flow on earth; and she haunted his beguiling streams. But in place of Enipeos, and in his likeness, there came the god [Poseidon] who sustains and who shakes the earth. He lay with her at the mouth of the eddying river, and a surging wave, mountain-high, curled over them and concealed the god and the mortal girl. And when the god had finished the work of love, he uttered these words with her hand in his: 'Girl, be happy in this our love. When the year comes round you will be the mother of glorious children (an immortal's embrace is not in vain); tend them and care for them. Now return home; be wary, and say no word of me **(Other translations say: *Do not say my name*)***; nevertheless I would have you know that I am the Shaker of the Earth, Poseidon. (Only for you, I am Poseidon, the Shaker of the Earth)"***

The Book of the Dead of ancient Egypt is very revealing too (Translation A. W. Budge):

31

May my name be proclaimed *when it is found upon the board of the table of offerings*

May my name be proclaimed*, may it be found, may it be lastingly renewed.*

(...)
His name *is honourable.*

(...)
Osiris, the favoured one of his divine city, triumphant, is known unto you ye worms and ***he knoweth your names.***

(...)
May offerings be made unto me in your presence, for I know you and ***I know your names,*** *and* ***I know the name*** *of the great god.*

(...)
May their knives never get the mastery over me, may I never fall under their instruments of cruelty, ***for I know their names,***

(...)
I have made my name to fourish, and I have delivered it, *that I may make myself to live in remembrance on this day.*

(...)
I live; and it liveth; I grow strong, I live, I sniff the air. I am the discriminator of Purity, or, as others say, ***the survivor whose name is pure;***

(...)

And cause ye not evil words to spring up against it; **because this heart of Osiris is the heart of the one of many names.**

Several questions are asked, and always, the one I will call later the "reincarnated" knows the answers, for example:

- Who then is this?
- "Devourer for millions of years" **is his name,** *and he dwelleth in the Lake of Unt.*

Or:

- What then is this?
- He seeth what is in his hand, **is the name of the shrine,** *or as others say,* **the name of the block.** *Now he whose mouth shineth and whose head moveth is a limb of Osiris, or as others say, of Ra.*
> **The name of the doorkeeper** *is Sekhet-hra-asht-aru, reversed of face (...)* »

In *Völuspá,* reported by Snorri Sturluson, there is also the occurrence of this system with the names of the dwarves. They are listed from *the 9th verse*:

9.
Þá gengu regin öll
á rökstóla,
ginnheilög goð,
ok um þat gættusk,
hverir skyldi dverga
dróttir skepja

ór Brimis blóði
ok ór Bláins leggjum.

10.
Þar var Móðsognir
mæztr of orðinn
dverga allra,
en Durinn annarr;
þeir mannlíkun
mörg of gerðu
dvergar í jörðu,
sem Durinn sagði.

11.
Nýi, Niði,
Norðri, Suðri,
Austri, Vestri,
Alþjófr, Dvalinn,
Nár ok Náinn
Nípingr, Dáinn
Bívurr, Bávurr,
Bömburr, Nóri,
Ánn ok Ánarr,
Óinn, Mjöðvitnir.

12.
Veggr ok Gandalfr,
Vindalfr, Þorinn,
Þrár ok Þráinn,
Þekkr, Litr ok Vitr,
Nýr ok Nýráðr,
nú hefi ek dverga,
Reginn ok Ráðsviðr,
rétt of talða.

13.
Fíli, Kíli,
Fundinn, Náli,
Hefti, Víli,
Hannar, Svíurr,
Billingr, Brúni,
Bíldr ok Buri,
Frár, Hornbori,
Frægr ok Lóni,
Aurvangr, Jari,
Eikinskjaldi.

14.
Mál er dverga
í Dvalins liði
ljóna kindum
til Lofars telja,
þeir er sóttu
frá salar steini
Aurvanga sjöt
til Jöruvalla.

15.
Þar var Draupnir
ok Dolgþrasir,
Hár, Haugspori,
Hlévangr, Glóinn,
Dóri, Óri
Dúfr, Andvari
Skirfir, Virfir,
Skáfiðr, Ái.

16.
Alfr ok Yngvi,
Eikinskjaldi,

Fjalarr ok Frosti,
Finnr ok Ginnarr;
þat mun æ uppi
meðan öld lifir,
langniðja tal
Lofars hafat.

What about the more recent name of **Perceval** by Chrétien de Troyes (What *Troyes* by the way?)? He remembers that after visiting the Fisher King, and that was the expected password:

And the boy, who didn't know his name, guessed and said it was Perceval the Welshman – *not knowing whether it was true or not. But it was true, though he didn't know it.*

What about the famous *"Pull the bobbin, and the latch will go up"* (password) that opens the house (grave) of the grandmother in the famous tale of *Little Red Riding Hood*. The seven names of the seven dwarfs in the tale of Snow White are also passwords to be known, like the names of the dwarves of *the Völuspá*. The names-passwords are always strange, just like a modern password will without any doubt be. They seem to be very strange to another person than yourself, because it must not be discovered by someone other than yourself, and it is a mixture of elements linked to your own unique memory.

Because you now know *why*, I'll explain *how*.

CHAPTER ONE
The Cake of Kings

We start early in the year.

In France, there is a tradition at Epiphany (January 6th), or after Christmas, where we eat a cake with a bean in it.

Ἐπιφάνεια/Epiphaneia means *manifestation* or *appearance*, from the verb φαίνω/Phaino: *to manifest, to appear obvious.*

The one who gets the bean becomes the king of the year and wears a crown on the head for the day. Generally it is a child. In other European countries there are similar traditions, sometimes there is more a porridge than a cake. Today, beans are often small subjects in porcelain, before they were just large beans.

This is the same bean as the magical beans in *Jack and the Beanstalk*. It is also the small white stones that *Little Tom Thumb* has sown behind him to find his way home. This is also the (gold) coin given to Charon to pass the Styx River. You will understand.
It is not that the one who finds the bean will become the king. In fact, it is he who loses his milk teeth during the year (which very often fall naturally by eating... in a cake, for example). It is this one who "become king" in fact: he will be rewarded with a crown (and even today also coins: we exchange milk teeth against coins.

Oh... In fact a mouse did this, *i. e.* an animal that digs in the soil, a symbol of the graves).

This crown is no other than, originally, horns, specifically horns from deer or reindeer. This is because the deer or reindeer horns are nothing but... the shovel of the Stone Age. We will talk more about that.

There was once upon a time a poor widow who had an only son named Jack, **and a cow named Milky-white. And all they had to live on was the milk the cow gave every morning,** *which they carried to the market and sold.* **But one morning Milky-white gave no milk, and they didn't know what to do.**

'What shall we do, what shall we do?' said the widow, wringing her hands.

'Cheer up, mother, I'll go and get work somewhere,' said Jack.

'We've tried that before, and nobody would take you,' said his mother; 'we must sell Milky-white and with the money start a shop, or something.'

'All right, mother,' says Jack; 'it's market-day today, and I'll soon sell Milky-white, and then we'll see what we can do.'

(Other translations report that the mother asks Jack to sell it for at least ten pieces of silver.)

So he took the cow's halter in his hand, and off he went. **He hadn't gone far before he met a funny-looking old man, who said to him: 'Good morning, Jack.'**

(This old man also knows the name of the boy...)

'Good morning to you,' said Jack, and wondered how he knew his name.

'Well, Jack, and where are you off to?' said the man.

'I'm going to the market to sell our cow.'

'Oh, you look the proper sort of chap to sell cows,' said the man; 'I wonder if you know how many beans make five.'

'Two in each hand and one in your mouth,' says Jack, as sharp as a needle.

'Right you are,' says the man, (Yes, Jack tells the truth because it's the password, not a mathematical exercise) **'and here they are, the very beans themselves,' he went on, pulling out of his pocket a number of strange-looking beans. 'Since you are so sharp,' says he, 'I don't mind doing a swop with you--your cow for these beans.'**

'Go along,' says Jack; 'wouldn't you like it?'

'Ah! you don't know what these beans are,' said the man; 'if you plant them overnight, by morning they grow right up to the sky.'

'Really?' said Jack; 'you don't say so.'

'Yes, that is so, and if it doesn't turn out to be true you can have your cow back.'

'Right,' says Jack, and hands him over Milky-white's halter and pockets the beans.

Back goes Jack home, and as he hadn't gone very far it wasn't dusk by the time he got to his door.

Jack and the beanstalk

Once upon a time there lived a woodcutter and his wife; they had seven children, all boys. The eldest was but ten years old, **and the youngest only seven.** People were astonished that the woodcutter had had so many children in such a short time, but his wife was very fond of children, **and never had less than two at a time.**

They were very poor, and their seven children inconvenienced them greatly, because not one of them was able to earn his own way. They were especially concerned, because the youngest was very sickly. He scarcely ever spoke a word, which they considered to be a sign of stupidity, although it was in truth a mark of good sense. **He was very little, and when born no bigger than one's thumb, for which reason they called him Little Thumb.**

The poor child bore the blame of everything that went wrong in the house. Guilty or not, he was always held to be at fault. He was, notwithstanding, more cunning and had a far greater share of wisdom than all his brothers put together. **And although he spoke little, he listened well.**

There came a very bad year, and the famine was so great that these poor people decided to rid themselves of their children. One evening, when the children were all in bed and the woodcutter was sitting with his wife at the fire, he said to her, with his heart ready to burst with grief, "You see plainly that we are not able to keep our children, and I cannot see them starve to death before my face. I am resolved to lose them in the woods tomorrow, which may very easily be done; for, while they are busy in tying up the bundles of wood, we can leave them, without their noticing."

"Ah!" cried out his wife; "and can you yourself have the heart to take your children out along with you on purpose to abandon them?"

In vain her husband reminded her of their extreme poverty. She would not consent to it. Yes, she was poor, but she was their mother. However, after having considered what a grief it would be for her to see them perish with hunger, she at last consented, and went to bed in tears.

Little Thumb heard every word that had been spoken; for observing, as he lay in his bed, that they were talking very busily, he got up softly, and hid under his father's stool, in order to hear what they were saying without being seen. He went to bed again, but did not sleep a wink all the rest of the night, thinking about what he had to do. He got up early in the morning, and went to the riverside, where he filled his pockets with small white pebbles, and then returned home.

They all went out, but Little Thumb never told his brothers one syllable of what he knew. They went into a very thick forest, where they could not see one another at ten paces distance. The woodcutter began his work, and the children gathered up the sticks into bundles. Their father and mother, seeing them busy at their work, slipped away from them without being seen, and returned home along a byway through the bushes.

When the children saw they had been left alone, they began to cry as loudly as they could. **Little Thumb let them cry, knowing very well how to get home again, for he had dropped the little white pebbles all along the way.** *Then he said to them, "Don't be afraid, brothers. Father and mother have left us here, but I will lead you home again. Just follow me."*

They did so, and he took them home by the very same way they had come into the forest. They dared not go in, but sat down at the door, listening to what their father and mother were saying.

Little Thumb *(by Charles Perrault)*

These first milk teeth fall to seven years. Yes, seven. At an age when the child, anthropologically, is weaned, that is why, in the tale of Jack, the mother's cow don't give milk anymore, it can hardly be more clear ... In the *Tom Thumb* fairy tale, the lack of food and abandonment is like weaning and gives way to the ancestor who comes through and by the new (adult) teeth.

Seven years, *the age of reason*, where the child's brain is roughly of the same size as the one of adults. This is also the age when the child is physically and scientifically reasonable, since he is then capable of inhibitions. He is able to not follow his impulses and automation. This new ability brought him out from the strict survival (which was up to now his first occupation) and made him an intelligent being.

It is the age of the first adult teeth, the ones I like to call *the teeth of the ancestors*. Yes, it is, in a way, the ancestor who grew up in the body of the child, who is none other than himself, re-born. This is also the age when the famous above-named crystallization is the strongest, or the need for ideal and for identification is the most important.

That is why it is an old man who gives the beans to Jack, and that is why Jack's father died (as often in these fairy tales): it is the image of the missing ancestor who returns.

Seven years is also the age of the footprints found in the caves of Pech Merle (-20,000, France) and Chauvet Pont d'Arc (-35,000, France). The only two footprints found in the decorated caves. These only two footprints had probably 15,000 years age difference, but both are of a child of about seven or eight years.

Seven, this is, you know, one of or the most common numbers in European traditions, in the legendary tales, in mythology, etc... I can not quote all references to the number seven in *the Iliad*, for example, but you will find that compared to my explanations, these multiple references in History and stories will turn out to be much more than details: they will receive their full meaning.

In *the Iliad*, Ajax, the Greek hero has a shield with seven skins of well-fed bulls. You will understand that the shield represents the womb of the pregnant mother, the life. It contracts itself to protect the fetus. The child is "finished" when weaned; seven years is a kind of second birth and especially when the ancestor took possession of his new body which is then anthropologically ready, independent, born and alive.

Sure, I will write about the famous seven dwarves. Not about a dwarf, because it will be explained later, but there are seven for the same reasons that *there are seven fathers in the house (Den syvende far i huset: The seventh father of the house*, a Norwegian traditional fairy tale transcribed by Asbjørnsen and Moe).

The seven dwarves, the seven fathers, who in this tale, when becoming older are also becoming smaller and childish, are undoubtedly the seven years of life. They are the representatives of the past seven years. So Snow White was seven. Similarly, the fact that there are seven children in the family of Tom Thumb, does not mean that there are seven children, but that there is in fact only one seven years old child.

There was once a man who traveling. He came, at last, to a beautiful. Big farm. It had a manor house so fine that it could easily have been a small castle. "This will be a good place to rest,» he said to himself as he went trough the gate. **An old man, with gray hair and beard, was chopping wood nearby.**

"Good evening, father" said the traveler. "Can you put me up for the night? " **I'm not the father of the house," said the old one. "Go into the kitchen and talk to my father". The traveler went into the kitchen. There he found a man who was even older, down on his knees in front of the hearth, blowing on the fire.**

"Good evening, father. Can you put me up for the night? " Said the traveler **"I'm not the father of the house," said the old fellow. "But go in and talk to my father. He's sitting by the table in the parlor".**

So the traveler went into the parlor and talked to the man who was sitting by the table.

He was much older than both the others were, and he sat, shivering and shaking, his teeth chattering, reading from a big book almost like a little child.

"Good evening, father. Will you put me up for the night?" said the man. **"I'm not the father of the house, but talk to my father, who's sitting on the settle," said the old man, who sat by the table, shivering and shaking, his teeth chattering. So the traveler went over to the one who was sitting on the settle, and he was busy trying to smoke a pipe of tobacco. But he was so huddled up, and his hands shook so that he could hardly hold onto the pipe.**

"Good evening, father," said the traveler again. "Can you put me up for the night?» **I'm not the father of the house," replied the huddled up old fellow, "But talk to my father who is lying in the bed". The traveler went over to the bed; and there lay and old, old man in whom there were no sign of life but a pair of big eyes.**

"Good evening, father. Can you put me up for the night?" said the traveler. **"I'm not the father of the house, but talk to my father who's lying in the cradle," said the man with the big eyes Well, the traveler went over to the cradle. There lay an ancient fellow, so shriveled up that he was no bigger than a baby was. And there was no way of telling there was life in him except for a rattle in his throat now and then.**

"Good evening, father. Can you put me up for the night?" asked the man. It took a long time before he got an answer, and even longer before the fellow finished it. **He said - he like all the others - that he was not the father of the house. "But talk to my father.**

He's hanging in the horn on the wall". The traveler stared up along the walls, and at last he caught sign of the horn, too. Bit when he tried to see the one who was lying in it, there was nothing to see but a little ash-white form that had the likeness of a human face. Then he was so frightened that he cried aloud:

"GOOD EVENING FATHER! WILL YOU PUT ME UP FOR THE NIGHT?" There was a squeaking sound up in the horn **like a tiny titmouse***, and it was all he could do to make out that the sound meant: "Yes, my child" Then in came a table decked with the costliest dishes, and with ale and spirits, too. And when the traveler had eaten and drunk, in came a good bed covered with reindeer hides.* **And he was very glad that at last he had found the true father of the house.**

The seventh Father of the House

The white stones and beans are the lost milk teeth. The number seven, is systematically representing the seven years. If we follow the Pagan traditions, adopted by the Christians, we are in the week with *the seven fat days* in February ended with *the Shrove Tuesday*. This name is very revealing. This is the seven days (years) with milk, when the child is fed handsomely.

This week therefore ends on the last day, on this Shrove Tuesday, where according to tradition, we eat some sweet food made with milk and eggs (pancakes, donuts), and especially where we disguise ourselves, i. e. we coat the personality of the ancestor who can now enter us in this alive and weaned body.

This Shrove Tuesday is followed by the Ash Wednesday, which is Pagan before being Christian. This is the recall of the ancestor or what remains of him from his grave (or his funeral pyre) into the child: his new body. This is the call of Cinderella (*Cinder* from French *cendres - ashes*), or the little Askeladden (*Aske*: ash *Askeladden*: the ash boy) in the Nordic folktales. Cinderella, Askeladden and all those other small heroes are sleeping or living in the ashes as they are the image of the dead ancestor. This is also why they often have ragged clothes and are sometimes relatively ugly and dirty (decomposed body).

The Ash Wednesday is for Christians (but, again, Christians have only taken again, willingly or unwillingly, the Pagan traditions) the beginning of the so well named Lent or *Carême* (from Latin *quaresima* or *quadragesima:* forty). In fact, during the Ash Wednesday, we should traditionally blow away the ashes or embers to revitalize the ancestor (by the blast, we can revive the fire, and give life to the dead).
What Cinderella and Askeladden are doing, that is just that, they take care of the fire, watch over the fire, blow to revive it. Through crystallization, the seven year old child, draws individuality and personality of the ancestor back to life. The ancestor enters his living and weaned body.

But then why Lent? Why forty days of fasting? Fasting? Not really. In fact the ancestor-child receives no solid food for forty days. You think this is strange, since he is weaned?

Yes... the ancestor-child lives another pregnancy, symbolically. In fact all these festivals maintain a permanent redundancy, or rather a repetition: three times. Three, and so forty, another frequent number in our myths, tales and traditions. Forty is for forty weeks: this is the forty weeks of pregnancy, from ovulation and fertilization until birth.

The ancestor-child is symbolically in a new pregnancy of forty weeks: the first of three new pregnancies before being fully reincarnated in his new body. In fact, he gets no more solid food, he "eats" nothing else than blood (in fact he does not even eat with the mouth ...).

Possibly, even surely, in the Stone Age, these traditions were followed by the seven years old child(ren) designated (i. e. the one(s) who had lost his (their) milk teeth). This only occurred one year in a life and was not followed by everyone, as it was a precise ritual concerning an individual.

These rituals have become traditions (more or less) followed by everyone. This first ritual of the Stone Age and these practices allowed the child to get out of childhood and put him in condition for his reincarnation and especially for his third symbolic pregnancy, which was the most difficult of all, and the one where he must gather all his strength and courage.

Christianity has made of ashes a symbol of our so-called sin, our human filth, that we are trying, they say, to repair during Lent. This notion of good and evil is a Christian attempt to dismantle the cyclical Pagan rites. It does not exist in the European, so-called Pagan religion.

The ashes represent the dead, the ancestor buried (or burned) and mainly consumed by time. They also represent the hidden embers in them, ready to relive, breathed on to be revived (in a new body, a living body, a breathing body). The ash is a good insulator to embers, but it is interesting, a good insulator and conservative at all: you can preserve eggs, dried meat and other foodstuffs in it.

Why the number three? Probably because there are three stages to be completed: the death, pregnancy and childbirth. Just as the moon, which must have three days to reappear. Historically and symbolically, it is always *three* for something to come back: the disappearance, the construction, the birth. This is the cycle, the circle, the formula to calculate the perimeter (the life) is, let us remember, the diameter multiplied by 3.14 (Pi).

Moreover, if we look at our traditional tales, where the action before the final success always occurs three times: the last of the three times is always a little longer because it includes success: life is somehow the famous 0.141592653589793 after three.... These stories are a kind of mythical Pi, that we finally "mathematified", quantified by numbers. That's why the number Pi was and is so important. It explains the inexplicable, life, eternity, infinity, and at the same time this cycle of rebirth.

Oh ! But Pi... Does not this remind you of anything? Pi is mystified today, but in fact, what is it for? To measure the perimeter of the circle. The way around the circle in fact.

Does it remind you of anything? In this book, I began by writing about time. In my first book (2009): *The need for the impossible*, that's what I wrote (p.59 / 60):

"As explained above, the so-called past is always projected into the present, or the present "reintegrates", "re-present", the "past" elements temporarily reserved in memory; likewise, what is called "future" is always a projection of the subject. From the three generally accepted "times" only the present is real, the other two are just illusory concepts to facilitate the use of the world, or life "in time" by the "present" person. If only the present, or more precisely the moment exists, then it is to understand how and why it seems to move to human eyes. If time had remained fixed, then it should be named as Eternity because it will then have no beginning nor end, neither past nor future.

No past, no future, no beginning and no end; it also what concerns human time, since past and future, as we just have demonstrated, are only illusions - or useful concepts, but illusory. Human time, this time, so is only and solely Eternity and Eternity loses its sense of "time out of the world" but is really in the world, intrinsic to time, the time of the world, and time or world itself, since the time is the world, and the world is the time.

So there is no eternity, no time, no separate world, but only Eternity.

Let us now compare Eternity, or the world, to an infinite and motionless ball, which we can call "the being Eternity". Seen through other eyes, prisoners of time, it becomes "the existing Eternity", that is to say, the moment, the present, moving in "time", or more accurately creating what is commonly called "the human time"."

The circle is infinite. It is this ball, which has suddenly been torn apart (they were my words, in 2009, when writing this book). The circle, here in two dimensions, is spread. Both when it is closed, and when it is spread, it contains Eternity. It contains death, construction and creation, and Eternity in the 0.141592653589793...

You know, we think the number Pi ($\pi\varepsilon\rho\acute{\iota}\mu\varepsilon\tau\rho o\varsigma$: *perimeter*) is infinite. In fact, it is so "infinite" that we are not even sure about that (yes, how to demonstrate the infinity in a finite world: this is just absurd...).

"The infinite" means "all-encompassing" and if we built an encrypted code based on our language (e. g, a = 1, b = 2 etc), so "infinite" would have meant that *everything is written in Pi*. You will find written your life in detail, it contains what I am writing now, the *Iliad* and the *Odyssey*, and all this in order and in all orders.

It contains my DNA, yours, the one of my children, those of my ancestors, those of your ancestors, those of your children. It is in front of this fact that the words "Infinity" or "Eternity" makes sense. Mathematics can not explain it, but there is infinitude in every circle or every sphere, small or large, it does not change anything. There is, as I presented it in 2009, Infinity, Eternity in every moment, and human time is just Eternity torn apart, spread out. This small 0.14... contains your life, mine, and all life, and our ancestors had understood.

Everything in the cottage was small, but neater and cleaner than can be told. There was a table on which was a white cover, and **seven little plates, and on each plate a little spoon, moreover, there were seven little knives and forks, and seven little mugs. Against the wall stood seven little beds side by side, and covered with snow-white counterpanes.**

Little Snow White was so hungry and thirsty that she ate some vegetables and bread from each plate and drank a drop of wine out of each mug, for she did not wish to take all from one only. Then, as she was so tired, she laid herself down on one of the little beds, **but none of them suited her, one was too long, another too short, but at last she found that the seventh one was right,** and so she remained in it, said a prayer and went to sleep.

Snow-White

Of course, in the story of Snow White, we find the number seven and beds, as bodies representing the various years. She lies down in the seventh bed: that means she is seven years old. The dwarf, meanwhile, is an image that comes up often. It represents the child-ancestor, so it is small, with an old man's head, it is the seven years old child with the head of the wise and dead ancestor, symbolically or least symbolically, since rituals from Stone Age and Neolithic show that the child was physically digging up the head or skull of the ancestor, we will see that later in the book.

The magician, with a symbol very close to the one of the dwarf, is the holder of the passwords and therefore he asks riddles to the child-ancestor to find out if he is really the right who is coming back. The magician and the dwarf have both the same type of hat. A rather pointed hat, often red. This is, in my opinion, the caul of the fetus in the womb: the amniotic sac.

Today the amniotic sac is often artificially punctured during childbirth, if not punctured naturally, and because of that are babies not often born "capped", but this was more common before. Yes, it is said of a child born with the amniotic sac on the head that he is "born with a caul", which refers to that hat in magicians or dwarves: that means a baby born with all or part of the amniotic sac on the head. We must also remember that a baby born vaginally often have a distorted head by the passage in the basin, and that is clearly or slightly pointed.

Babies born with a caul have always received special treatment, the superstition wanted them to have special powers, and before, it was the way (among other things) magicians were chosen.

This is a sign of belonging to the beyond, and therefore the child-ancestor has that hat on the head: this ritual and these stories about reincarnation happen in what is commonly called the afterlife and especially as it is a rebirth, this is the stage of pregnancy: the construction.

Viel Glück
im neuen Jahre!

CHAPTER TWO
The bird and the eggs

She immediately ran to open the door, and said, hugging them, "I am so glad to see you, my dear children; you are very hungry and tired. And my poor Peter, you are horribly dirty; come in and let me clean you."

Now, you must know that Peter was her eldest son, whom she loved above all the rest, because he had red hair, as she herself had.

They sat down to have supper and ate with a good appetite, which pleased both father and mother. They told them how frightened they had been in the forest, speaking almost always all together. *The parents were extremely glad to see their children once more at home,* **and this joy continued while the ten crowns lasted;** *but, when the money was all gone, they fell again into their former uneasiness, and decided to abandon them again. This time they resolved to take them much deeper into the forest than before.*

Although they tried to talk secretly about it, again they were overheard by Little Thumb, who made plans to get out of this difficulty as well as he had the last time. **However, even though he got up very early in the morning to go and pick up some little pebbles, he could not do so, for he found the door securely bolted and locked.**

Their father gave each of them a piece of bread for their breakfast, and he fancied he might make use of this instead of the pebbles, by throwing it in little bits all along the way; and so he put it into his pocket.

Their father and mother took them into the thickest and most obscure part of the forest, then, slipping away by an obscure path, they left them there. Little Thumb was not concerned, for he thought he could easily find the way again by means of his bread, which he had scattered along the way; but he was very much surprised when he could not find so much as one crumb. **The birds had come and had eaten every bit of it up.** *They were now in great distress, for the farther they went the more lost and bewildered they became.*

Night now came on, and there arose a terrible high wind, which made them dreadfully afraid. **They fancied they heard on every side of them the howling of wolves coming to eat them up. They scarcely dared to speak or turn their heads. After this, it rained very hard, which drenched them to the skin; their feet slipped at every step they took, and they fell into the mire, getting them muddy all over. Their hands were numb with cold.**

Tom Thumb

Well, I have taken these examples, and there are many others, as you know. I want you to notice that *the details are important, and are not there by chance*, but they are well placed there by our ancestors, *in the hope that we understand the real meaning of the story.* Take this:

"- If you like, but you must request at least ten pieces of silver." (*Jack and the Beanstalk*) and "*The parents were extremely glad to see their children once more at home, and this joy continued while the ten crowns lasted*" (Tom Thumb). Why ten in both cases? In stories which, *a priori*, don't have anything in common (when in fact they tell the same thing)?

There are two possible reasons:

Because ten: 10, it is after nine: 9, after nine months (of pregnancy), it is the birth, and in numerology a new beginning, since we begin the dozens. So in ten (birth, life), we start a new pregnancy.

But also... Because 10 is 10 times 28, 10 female cycles, it is 280 days, the time of pregnancy. Before, there were calendars with 13 months of 28 days (Varg Vikernes, *Sorcery and Religion in Ancient Scandinavia*). I will call that calendar the moon (or woman) or ancient calendar, and the other (the one with 12 months) the solar (4 seasons divided each in 3 months) or modern calendar. I believe they used both before. So 10 is the tenth month, the latest in a pregnancy, just before birth.

In the story of Tom Thumb, we enter here in the second pregnancy-reincarnation. The first pregnancy, fairly simple and relatively short can be summarized thus: weaning and tooth loss (kings cake, bean) and seven fat days ending with the seventh day: the carnival, which invite the ancestor in his new body through the interest of the child.

The following Ash Wednesday marks the reappearance of the ancestor on which we "breathe" as on insulated embers in the ashes. Then come the forty days of fasting-pregnancy (the second), and the (second) birth: directly engaged in the symbolic third pregnancy (the circle have no cut, all is attached and nested one inside the other).

In the tale of *Hansel and Gretel*, which is very close to that of Tom Thumb, it is told this at the time of "the second pregnancy," that is to say, in the tales, when the action is repeated for the second time:

At daybreak, even before sunrise, the woman came and woke the two children. "Get up, you lazybones. You are going into the woods to fetch wood." Then she gave each one a little piece of bread, saying, "Here is something for midday. Don't eat it any sooner, for you'll not get any more."
On the way to the woods, Hansel crumbled his piece in his pocket, then often stood still, and threw crumbs onto the ground.

When they were deep into the woods, a large fire was made, and the father said, "Sit here, children. If you get tired you can sleep a little. I am going into the woods to cut wood. I will come and get you in the evening when I am finished."

When it was midday Gretel shared her bread with Hansel, who had scattered his piece along the path. Then they fell asleep, and evening passed, but no one came to get the poor children.

When the moon appeared they got up, but they could not find any crumbs, for the many thousands of birds that fly about in the woods and in the fields had eaten them. They walked through the entire night and the next day from morning until evening, but they did not find their way out of the woods.

They were terribly hungry, for they had eaten only a few small berries that were growing on the ground. And because they were so tired that their legs would no longer carry them, they lay down under a tree and fell asleep.

It was already the third morning since they had left the father's house. They started walking again, but managed only to go deeper and deeper into the woods. If help did not come soon, they would perish. **At midday they saw a little snow-white bird sitting on a branch.** *It sang so beautifully that they stopped to listen. When it was finished it stretched its wings and flew in front of them.*

Hansel and Gretel

In the tale of *Jack and the Beanstalk* it is told as thus:

So they lived on the bag of gold for some time, but at last they came to the end of it, and Jack made up his mind to try his luck once more at the top of the beanstalk. So one fine morning he rose up early, and got on to the beanstalk, and he climbed and he climbed and he climbed and he climbed and he climbed and he climbed till at last he came out on to the road again and up to the great tall house he had been to before. There, sure enough, was the great tall woman a-standing on the doorstep.

'Good morning, mum,' says Jack, as bold as brass, 'could you be so good as to give me something to eat?'

'Go away, my boy,' said the big tall woman, 'or else my man will eat you up for breakfast. But aren't you the youngster who came here once before? Do you know, that very day my man missed one of his bags of gold.'

'That's strange, mum,' said Jack, 'I dare say I could tell you something about that, but I'm so hungry I can't speak till I've had something to eat.'

Well, the big tall woman was so curious that she took him in and gave him something to eat. But he had scarcely begun munching it as slowly as he could when thump! thump! they heard the giant's footstep, and his wife hid Jack away in the oven.

All happened as it did before. In came the ogre as he did before, said: 'Fee-fi-fo-fum', and had his breakfast off three broiled oxen. Then he said: 'Wife, bring me the hen that lays the golden eggs.' So she brought it, and the ogre said: 'Lay,' and it laid an egg all of gold.

And then the ogre began to nod his head, and to snore till the house shook.

Then Jack crept out of the oven on tiptoe and caught hold of the golden hen, and was off before you could say 'Jack Robinson'. But this time the hen gave a cackle which woke the ogre, and just as Jack got out of the house he heard him calling:

'Wife, wife, what have you done with my golden hen?' And the wife said: 'Why, my dear?'

But that was all Jack heard, for he rushed off to the beanstalk and climbed down like a house on fire. And when he got home he showed his mother the wonderful hen, and said 'Lay' to it; and it laid a golden egg every time he said 'Lay.'

(Other versions speak of a goose)

Jack and the Beanstalk

It was too early in the day,
he left and did not seize his prey.
The young knight saw the goose was stranded
and galloped toward the place she landed.
Hurt in the neck, the goose had shed
three drops of crimson blood, which spread
like blushes on the clear white snow.
The goose was not hurt by the blow
and could still rise above the ground.
When Perceval arrived, he found
the goose had flown away again.
He saw the place the goose had lain;

the snow was pressed down when he found it,
with drops of crimson blood around it,
and started leaning on his lance
to contemplate them from this stance.
The blood and snow, both in one place,
made him recall his lady's face,
the colors of her bright complexion.
So Perceval fell in reflection
till he forgot himself outright.
The red contrasted with the white
complexion of his lady-love
in the same way the three drops of
red blood contrasted with the snow.
The combination pleased him so,
he thought he saw the colors clear
upon the face of one so dear.

Perceval

65

Geese and swans are birds with equivalent symbolism (placenta and cord). Likewise the storks that bring the children.

All these tales speak of a bird when they talk about what I call the second pregnancy. And it is a good thing.

Yes, it is good because in our tradition we are now at Easter. Easter is the birth of the first pregnancy (after 40 days, that means symbolically 40 weeks), hence the frequent image of the lamb: the newborn; and it is also the beginning of the second, nested within the first birth.

At the beginning of the new pregnancy, we recognize several things. First, Easter is nine months before Yule or Christmas, marking the birth of this pregnancy, especially, we shall see. And then there are the eggs, an avatar of the tree fruits.

The eggs are hidden, because at first they are so small they are almost invisible. They are hidden *by the mother (as in the womb)* and then sought and then found by children.

They represent two things: again the child who feeds with exterior products, because he is now seven years old and weaned, and the ancestor who "eats" an egg, representing both the body of re-birth and food, that means the fruit of the tiny "placenta" of early pregnancy. In many European countries, these eggs are decorated, often in red (red ocher, Slavic countries). This when there is no red egg in Nature, since they must be well camouflaged and well protected from predators.

This is because the egg at Easter represents the bloody fruit of the placenta, the food from the tree-Placenta. This tradition of decorating and offering eggs is so old that no one knows where it comes from. It is generally explained by the arrival of spring. Like almost all European and so-called Pagan traditions, it is always explained with the seasons. Of course, egg and spring are linked, not least because migratory birds loudly come back at this season, but this is not the egg that is used to symbolize the return of spring, it's spring which brings the symbolism of the egg.

I mean here that these traditions linked to three pregnancies and reincarnation of the ancestor in a new body alive and weaned, fetch their symbols in the seasons and the surrounding world, they are of course interlinked in the year, and that is why in this pregnancy, the symbol of the fruit of the tree-placenta is not a fruit (an apple), but an egg.

It can also be a flower (from spring), a red flower, such as a rose, as in *the Beauty and the Beast* story, which tells the same story:

One day, his father lost his entire fortune. *He and his daughters moved into a small Countryside house.*

On Ash Wednesday (The day after Shrove Tuesday - the first birth - and the beginning of Lent for Christians - forty days of partial fasting until Easter), the father-ancestor die, and he will be fed very little (he only drinks, blood in fact), during forty weeks, that means a whole pregnancy.

The family had lived about a year in this retirement, when the merchant received a letter with an account that a vessel, on board of which he had effects, was safely arrived. This news had liked to have turned the heads of the two eldest daughters, who immediately flattered themselves with the hopes of returning to town, for they were quite weary of a country life; and when they saw their father ready to set out, they begged of him to buy them new gowns, headdresses, ribbons, and all manner of trifles; but Beauty asked for nothing for she thought to herself, that all the money her father was going to receive, would scarce be sufficient to purchase everything her sisters wanted.

"What will you have, Beauty?" said her father.

"Since you have the goodness to think of me," she answered, "be so kind to bring me a rose, for as none grows hereabouts, they are a kind of rarity." Not that Beauty cared for a rose, but she asked for something, lest she should seem by her example to condemn her sisters' conduct, who would have said she did it only to look particular.

The good man went on his journey, but when he came there, they went to court with him about the merchandise, and after a great deal of trouble and pains to no purpose, he came back as poor as before.

He was within thirty miles of his own house, thinking of the pleasure he should have in seeing his children again, when going through a large forest he lost himself. It rained and snowed terribly; next to him, the wind was so strong, that it threw him twice off his horse, and night coming on, he began to apprehend being either starved to death with cold and hunger, or else devoured by the wolves, whom he heard howling all round him, when, all of a sudden, looking through a long walk of trees, he saw a light at some distance, and going on a little farther saw it came from a palace illuminated from top to bottom. God thanks for this happy discovery! He hastened to the palace, but was greatly surprised by not being met by any one in the outer courts.

His horse followed him, and seeing a large stable open, he went in, and finding both hay and oats, the poor beast, who was almost famished, fell to eating very heartily; the merchant tied him up to the manger, and walking towards the house, where he saw no one, but entering into a large hall, he found a good fire, and a table plentifully set out with but one cover laid. *As he was wet quite through with the rain and snow, he drew near the fire to dry himself. "I hope," said he, "the master of the house, or his servants will excuse the liberty I take; I suppose it will not be long before some of them appear."*

He waited a considerable time, until the clock struck eleven, and still nobody came. At last he was so hungry that he could stay no longer, but took a chicken, and ate it in two mouthfuls, trembling all the while. After this he drank a few glasses of wine, and growing more courageous he went out of the hall, and crossed through several grand apartments with magnificent furniture, until he came into a chamber, which had an exceeding good bed in it, and as he was very much fatigued, and it was past midnight, he concluded it was best to shut the door, and go to bed.

First pregnancy and first birth especially: in the twelfth month of the year he is eating or drinking milk in abundance, and then returns to his death.

It was ten a clock the next morning before the merchant woke up, and as he was going to rise he was astonished to see a good suit of clothes in the room of his own, which were quite spoiled; certainly, said he, this palace belongs to some kind fairy, who has seen and pitied my distress.

He looked through a window, but instead of snow saw the most delightful arbors, interwoven with the most beautifull flowers that were ever beheld. He then returned to the great hall, where he had eaten the night before, and found some chocolate ready made on a little table. "Thank you, good Madam Fairy," said he aloud, "for being so careful, as to provide me a breakfast; I am extremely obliged to you for all your favors."

The good man drank his chocolate, and then went to look for his horse, but ***passing through an arbor of roses he remembered Beauty's request to him, and gathered a branch on which were several; immediately he heard a great noise, and saw such a frightful Beast coming towards him,*** *that he was ready to faint away.*

"You are very ungrateful," said the Beast to him, in a terrible voice; "I have saved your life by receiving you into my castle, and, in return, you steal my roses, which I value beyond any thing in the universe, but you shall die for it; ***I give you but a quarter of an hour to prepare yourself, and say your prayers."***

"A quarter (4) of an hour" is probably a reference to the number forty.

The merchant fell on his knees, and lifted up both his hands, ***"My lord," said he, "I beseech you to forgive me, indeed I had no intention to offend in gathering a rose for one of my daughters, who desired me to bring her one."***

"My name is not My Lord," replied the monster, "but Beast; I don't love compliments, not I. I like people to speak as they think; and so do not imagine, I am to be moved by any of your flattering speeches. **But you say you have got daughters. I will forgive you, on condition that one of them come willingly, and suffer for you. Let me have no words, but go about your business, and swear that if your daughter refuse to die in your stead, you will return within three months."**

The merchant had no mind to sacrifice his daughters to the ugly monster, but he thought, in obtaining this respite, he should have the satisfaction of seeing them once more, so he promised, upon oath, he would return, and the Beast told him he might set out when he pleased, **"but,"** he added, **"you shall not depart empty handed; go back to the room where you lay, and you will see a great empty chest; fill it with whatever you like best, and I will send it to your home,"** and at the same time Beast withdrew.

"Well," said the good man to himself, "if I must die, I shall have the comfort, at least, of leaving something to my poor children." He returned to the bedchamber, and finding a great quantity of broad pieces of gold, he filled the great chest the Beast had mentioned, locked it, and afterwards took his horse out of the stable, leaving the palace with as much grief as he had entered it with joy. The horse, of his own accord, took one of the roads of the forest, and in a few hours the good man was at home.

The Beauty and the Beast

Instant start of the second pregnancy, nested in the birth of the first: the child-ancestor picks a rose, which is the same symbol as the red egg, red fruit of the tree-placenta, but in spring: he picks up the blood that will nourish it. The three months, likely are referring to three pregnancies, the french version are talking about eight days : the eight months remaining until the ninth: the birth. The second pregnancy is symbolized by the number nine, for nine months until birth, until Christmas/Yule.

(Remember that sometimes the number 9 is replaced by the number 10, as 10x28, 10 female cycles, 280 being the number of days in a pregnancy, and old calendars had 13 months of 28 days, or 13 female cycles. The pregnancy lasted therefore 10 months of 28 days.)

Concerning the horse, we will explain its meaning and its avatars (Unicorn, Pegasus, Trojan horse) at the end of this book. However, I must point out another element: the chest. You must understand that "the Beast" is the mother. The mother-bear, the one *bearing* (we shall see later that the English words "bear" and "to bear" have the same origin and are in a way synonyms).

The mother gives a chest to the ancestor-father-placenta-fetus (the old man). Strange? In fact not. The mother gives the egg, the ovary. Well, do you know what the amniotic bags, or rather one of the two amniotic sacs (because there are two: *the amnion*, of fetal origin, and *the chorion* or *lamina propria*, the mother ovular membrane)? It is the membrane of the ovule which has been considerably enlarged.

It's him, the chest. It is also the chest of the goddess Idun (the one who rejuvenates, who renews), in which she hides the rejuvenating apples allowing the gods to revive or rejuvenate... It is also the Santa's hood... This magic "bag" is like an egg, it is an egg, since it is in fact the ovule, and therefore the fetus is a bird.

Physically, this bag is a part of the placenta and is directly attached to the fetal face.

Note the meaning of "hood" which is none other than "hut", *i.e.* a bedroom, a cabin, a small house.

From Gothic hēþjō ("chamber") of the Indo-European root [s] keu- * ("surround, cover"). In this regard, see the words *hytte* (cottage, cabane) in Norwegian / Danish, or *hydda* (cottage, cabin) in Swedish, But also the blind Scandinavian god Höd, who is none other than the avatar of the placenta (always *the twin*), the brother of Baldr (the white god, that is to say the newborn, *like Snow White*, we shall see later that he is white as snow because of the *vernix caseosa*, produced by the amnion to protect the skin of the baby). Baldr is the one on which Höd shoot an arrow of mistletoe (the umbilical cord) by mistake, pushed by Loki. Höd (identical etymology to the word *hette*: *hood*, in Norwegian, is also called *Ull*: *wool, cover*, which clearly suggests this idea of something that covers, hides and protects: See Sorcery *and Religion in Ancient Scandinavia*, by Varg Vikernes). Höd is blind because his eyes are hidden by a cap (the water bag, the egg), like the fetus, he can not see the outside world with his eyes.

The bag

But that's not all. There is a god, a brother of Baldr (and of Höd) who is born solely to avenge the death of his brother Baldr: he is Vali. The name means "chosen" and "fallen", perhaps from the same etymology as the Latin *vale* meaning *"hello"* from *valeo, valere: to be strong, to be vigorous, to be in good health* (so: *to be alive*), *being powerful, having power*. This word has given the verb *valoir* (*to be worth*) in French.

In my opinion, the etymology of *Vali* can be compared to that of the word *valley* or *val*. From the Latin *vallis* (*valley*), coming from *vola* (*hollow*), common Indo-European *uel- (*"turn, round, round"*), see Latin *volva* (*"vulva"*) and *vulva* (*"womb"*), *vallus* (*"palisade"*) and even volvo. In other words, the same etymology as *valley* and *vulva*, with the same meaning as in Perceval (*pierce valley*): *the one that came out of the womb, the one that went through the vulva.*

Let us note that these two etymologies can themselves flow from the same root. ***Perceval is Vali, Vali Perceval.***

Still, Vali is a god created to avenge Baldr, killed by Hödr, killed by the umbilical cord. Interestingly, it is stated in Nordic mythology that he does not wash himself or combs hair until he has accomplished his task. *There, it was obvious*, Vali is the newborn, and also the living man before death or rebirth, or the child before seven years and the symbolic reincarnation.

He does not wash means that he does not get into the water bag in the womb, and he does not comb his hair means that he does not fit into the water bag, he is not "capped". You don't believe me ? You think I'm exaggerating? And yet, in the poem *Baldr draumar*, it is specified that he is only a day old (the newborn, the life) when he avenges Baldr:

11.
«Rindr berr Vala
i væstrsolvm,
sa man Oðins sonr
æinnættr væga:
hond vm þvær
næ hofvð kæmbir,
aðr a bal vm berr
Balldrs andskota;.

11.
"Rind bears Vali
in Vestrsalir,
And one night old
fights Othin's son;
His hands he shall not wash ,
his hair he shall not comb,
Till the slayer of Baldr
he brings to the flames.

In *Little Thumb* (or *Tom Thumb*), in addition to the picture of the bird that ate bread crumbs, the description of pregnancy is clear:

They scarcely dared to speak or turn their heads. After this, it rained very hard, which drenched them to the skin; their feet slipped at every step they took, and they fell into the mire, getting them muddy all over. Their hands were numb with cold.

(This is the version from Charles Perrault, in French literally it is written: *they did not know what to do with their hands.*)

As in all stories, in all myths, we have the symbol of water. The powerful water, which eats, kills or drowns the body, which encircles and contains it. It is the water in the womb, the amniotic fluid, the water that literally pierces the bones. Here, it is moreover said "*They scarcely dared to speak or turn their heads.* "(...)"*they did not know what to do with their hands.*" Why? Why if the tale just mean what it is written? On the other hand, if it describes the child or the children in the womb, the image can be understood.

If the egg is the symbol of this pregnancy, then the child-fetus is the bird, the bird, the fairy (Cinderella, Rapunzel) or the bee, since the egg-symbol can also be the flower (The object of reproduction which needs to be fertilized), the tree, the rose bush being a small tree (*rosa canina*). We already know that Neandertal used corvid and raptor feathers. (See *Birds of a Feather: Neanderthal Exploitation of Raptors and Corvids*, study dated from October 2012)

Pharaoh, on the other hand, possessed a cap adorned with a bird (nothing astonishing since it was assimilated to Horus) or... the well-known blue and gold cap, the *Nemes*, like the bees. Bees also naturally produce "houses" in the trunks of trees, that is to say trunks of trees full of honey.

That is to say, since the tree trunk is the avatar of the umbilical cord, honey is the avatar of the blood, and the bees are certainly the ones that nourish, but above all, it is often forgotten: the fed ones. (Honey is made by but especially for the bees themselves, which eat it during the winter). In other words, the fetus of this pregnancy is symbolized by the bee or the bird.

Mask of Tutankhamon with the gold and blue Nemes. The protective snake, the uraeus, is clearly positioned on the forehead.

The avatars are many. They are not always related to a particular pregnancy. The placenta has its own, the main one: the tree, the ramifications. The umbilical cord is the trunk and are many others avatars that you will recognize very quickly: the snake for example.

On this subject, I will tell you a story. I did not invent it, I draw it from one of the most famous books in the world, and one of the oldest, and you will see it tells many things. This is the Iliad. The different translations give either a dragon with a bloody back or a snake with a red back.

We were ranged round about a fountain offering hecatombs to the gods upon their holy altars, and there was a fine plane-tree from beneath which there welled a stream of pure water. Then we saw a sign [sêma]; for Zeus sent a fearful serpent out of the ground, with blood-red stains upon its back, and it darted from under the altar on to the plane-tree. Now there was a brood of young sparrows, quite small, upon the topmost bough, peeping out from under the leaves, eight in all, and their mother that hatched them made nine. The serpent ate the poor cheeping things, while the old bird flew about lamenting her little ones; but the serpent threw his coils about her and caught her by the wing as she was screaming. Then, when he had eaten both the sparrow and her young, the god who had sent him made him become a sign; for the son of scheming Kronos turned him into stone, and we stood there wondering at that which had come to pass. Seeing, then, that such a fearful portent had broken in upon our hecatombs, Kalkhas forthwith declared to us the oracles of heaven.

'Why, Achaeans,' said he, 'are you thus speechless? Zeus has sent us this sign, long in coming, and long ere it be fulfilled, though its fame [kleos] shall last for ever. As the serpent ate the eight fledglings and the sparrow that hatched them, which makes nine, so shall we fight nine years at Troy, but in the tenth shall take the town.'

Homer, *The Iliad*

Does the snake or dragon really eat the birds (avatars of the fetus, the child in the tree) in the tree? Yes and no. Symbolically yes, but in fact, it clings to them, as the umbilical cord clings to the fetus, already next to the future placenta. It bites him in the belly, sometimes it sends him his venom, avatar of the blood, and sometimes his fire, for the dragon is also an avatar of the umbilical cord, and the fire of venom and therefore blood.

Fire, light, blood and... sugar (or food) are all avatars of blood. They are because in practice it is the same thing: energy. All energy comes from light and therefore is light, it is simply "preserved" in the form of blood, sugar, or wood (fire) as in batteries, but it is always the energy of the sun and stars: light, The only possible source of the energy of life.

Remember: trees and plants are only the first step in conserving energy because the whole food chain is a form of energy conservation: they use light to transform the elements.

The light is used to transform carbon into wood, and is therefore itself transformed into wood and/or vegetable food, and consumed, and then transformed either into heat energy or nutrients for the soil or into blood. After that, the blood is transformed into blood again or into nutrients for the soil to be consumed again by the plants.

The venom now is also an avatar of blood and paradoxically of life, for the one who gives life inevitably gives death, he gives the venom of the first *sickness unto death.*

The umbilical cord is also the holder of the magic, the magic of the beginning of life. What is interesting is that umbilical cord blood is *actually* "magical", it can cure otherwise nearly incurable diseases like leukemia because it contains stem cells, but it is especially the one that gives life again and again.

This umbilical cord often has as avatar beard or hair, as in the tale of Rapunzel or the myth of Medusa, but also everything that looks like it: a belt, a lace, a garland, a necklace, or even a branch of mistletoe. Indeed, mistletoe is "bitten" in the tree: this is maybe the most obvious symbol, which explains its sacredness.

Maybe this will surprise you, but you will see later that this is right: the king's scepter, or the sorcerer's staff is also an avatar of the umbilical cord. The spear too, sometimes. And look carefully at this painting:

"The Well", Lascaux (-18,000), France

Does not that remind you of something? The eaten birds eaten from the Iliad. This is not the only time the scepter is surmounted by a bird. The scepter of Zeus is also decorated with a bird, or it is accompanied by it, and that of Óðinn/Hermes has two snake heads and feathers.

Okay, but let's stop there, because now it's about proving what I'm saying. Do not care who died and why, or who will live again.

You will have to follow.

In the tale of Jack ..., the tree and its cord are the giant bean. In Tom Thumb, the boy climbs a tree to see far away. In the tale of Beauty and the Beast, Beauty's father plucks a rose from the tree. In Snow White's tale, it is the whole forest (as in Tom Thumb's tale) that acts as a tree and a placenta (since the individual in the tree world does not exist strictly speaking, and a whole forest can be genetically a single tree, and come from a single seed, this image is not shocking).

In the tale of Rapunzel, the hair is the cord (which hangs her on to her stepmother), and the tower is the avatar of the immense tree from which she can not climb down from, and of which she is a prisoner, like the fetus in the womb. This symbol is present every time, but for now and with only these elements it will not always be easy to understand.

Of course, it is the same tree than the one in Paradise, and the same serpent, the same fruit.

Of course, it's the same World Tree (*Yggdrasil*) in Norse mythology, the tree on which Óðinn remains hung, blind (fetus) pierced with a spear during *nine days and nine nights* (so nine months: time the pregnancy).

Of course, the tree, the cord is the spear in the cave of Lascaux (-17,000, France), it is also the same spear in the tale of Perceval, the bleeding spear (supposedly the one that touched Christ, id est the fetus). The spear clings to the fetus and pierces it, as the serpent bites it.

This tree is the Yule tree or so-called Christmas tree, not originally a fir tree, but an yew tree (*taxus baccata*), a sacred tree, a symbol of eternity, neither hardwood nor conifer, a single tree , With evergreen leaves, but a classic form of tree, with strange red blood berries, incomparable taste when mature, incredibly sweet and *honeyed*, while the rest of the tree is so toxic it is deadly. There is in this tree a summary of what I describe in this book. The venom/sweet food duality is one, but also immortality/reincarnation and the connection between placenta/cordon and lance/weapon, because yew was the essence of choice for all weapons in history (bows, but also arrows, spears, etc.).

Of course, in the myth of Atlantis, in the Atlas Island (Plato, *The Critias*), the placenta-cordon-tree, is the column in the center of the city, on which are sacrificed bulls, so on which the blood flows, that blood that nourishes the fetus.

It is also the serpent on the head of the Pharaohs, *the uraeus*, the one who produces the scar of the symbolic pregnancy: *the third eye, the navel of the head*, in a way, the trace of the ancestor's coming into the head of the child. It is of course the serpent that adorns the neck of *the Kumari*, the virgin, the child goddess of Nepal.

This third eye is probably inspired by the pink task (hemangioma on the forehead), present on the majority of white pale babies at birth. It is also called "angel kiss birthmark", which makes the thoughts wander.

Let us recall that this "third" eye often possesses the elongated shape of the "angel kiss birthmark", and that it is red. Even the Kumari has the front entirely painted in red. Let us call it *the navel of the soul*, or *the bite of the serpent*. Remember that *the uraeus* of Pharaohs is also... the eye of Ra, and it can take the appearance of a woman, or a lioness.

The living goddess Kumari in Nepal, recognized and worshiped by both Buddhists and Hindus. The main color is red, the front paint is red, the coat is red and gold. She possesses a necklace in the shape of a snake around the neck, the most important attribute. The third eye is always marked or drawn on her forehead.

But we will go round in circles, because I can not quote all our myths, and yet everything overlaps, so we have to stop here, to talk about something else now.

So, when the tale says that the little Red Riding Hood is the little Red Riding Hood, you must not believe it. When the tale says that Snow White is Snow White, it should not be believed. When the tale says that Cinderella is Cinderella, it should not be believed. When he says Jack is Jack, don't believe it, Perceval Perceval, and so on.

Yes, because Little Red Riding Hood is her dead grandmother (in the tale she is sick and bedridden, meaning dead, buried); Snow White is her dead mother; Cinderella too. Jack is obviously his dead father, as well as Perceval, and so on. Hansel and Gretel, who is almost the same story as Tom Thumb his two faces of the same ancestor: the dead parents, because very poor, so poor that they can scarcely feed themselves (poverty is an image of death).

We might think that this is a teenage ritual, and in fact, as I have pointed out to you earlier, it is not. It is about a weaned child. About seven years old. But more than that... We have seen that this child was going through one (in fact three) symbolic pregnancy, or rather that the ancestor was revived in the child (his new body) in one/three symbolic pregnancy/pregnancies to be given birth in his new body, to be delivered. So this young child in stories *is a fetus*.

You will see how it is right, and as this always explains many details. Strange details, sometimes only kept in some local versions, because just too weird to be included in the official version. As proof, this excerpt from a local version of Little Red Riding Hood collected in Touraine (France) by M. Légot, and published in *La revue de l'Avranchin* in 1885:

He (described as a very ugly man) killed the poor woman and **poured her blood into a bottle ("huche" in French),** *stuck it in the cupboard, and got into bed.*

When the little girl arrived at her grandmother's house, she knocked at the door, opened it, entered, and said: How are you doing, grandma?"

"Not well, my daughter," responded the good-for-nothing who gave the impression that he was suffering and disguised his voice. **"Are you hungry?" "Yes, grandma. What's there to eat?"**

"There's some blood in the cupboard. Take the pan and fry it. Then eat it up."

The little girl obeyed.

(...)
While she was frying the blood, she heard some voices that sounded like those of angels from the top of the chimney, and they said: "Ah! Cursed be the little girl who's frying the blood of her grandmother!"

"What are those voices saying, grandmother those voices that are singing from the chimney?"

"Don't listen to them, my daughter, **those are just little birds singing in their own language."**

(...)
Jeannette became scared and said: "Ah! Grandmother, **I've got the urge to go (take a leak)."**

"Do it in bed, my daughter. Do it in bed."

"It would be too dirty, grandma! If you're afraid that I might run off, tie a rope around my leg. If you're bothered that I'm outside too long, just pull on the rope, and you can assure yourself that I'm still here."

"You're right my daughter. You're right."

(...)
The monster pulled the rope, but there was no one at the other end.

(...)
"Have you seen that Tomboy girl (or boy-girl)
With a dog wagging its tail
Tagging along on this trail?"

in French:
Avez-vous vu passer fillon fillette,
Avec un chien barbette (barbet)
Qui la suivette (suivait)

Little Red Riding Hood is called "Tomboy girl" (in French: *"fillon fillette"*, what means literally *"boy girl"*), not only she often (in many versions) does not have any name (like *Perceval*, like... babies in the womb, who are not yet born), but it is not clear whether it is a girl or a boy. Strange, disturbing... Unless it is a fetus (the wool rope is obviously the umbilical cord). Similarly, Hansel and Gretel are not two children, they are t*wo versions of one and the same child,* or the fetus (Hansel) and his twin: the placenta (Gretel): this is why their names are so similar (in French they are sometimes called *Jeannot* and *Margot*), and that they are the same age (they are twins).

The virgin, in traditions, is represented by a pubescent but young woman, and it is believed that virgin means *"untouched"* sexually speaking. In fact it is not the case, as you will see: originally, the virgin is a young girl, a little girl, who represents the fetus. Generally a little *girl*, because what happens in the womb of a woman is of course seen as very feminine; but she can be a little boy, this doesn't matter because we don't know. It is a secret until birth. We don't know the sex of the fetus, however, *initially it is always visually feminine.* The virgin represents the life, the embryo, the fetus. And this is all the more interesting when one notices that the etymology of "virgin" does not mean what we seems to believe today but *comes from the Latin* **virgo, virge**, this word means **"force", "life", "who is fed"** and in particular gave the word **"vigor"**. The virgin is the one who gives life, in whom life is shown; the virgin, the fetus, *is* life. She has not yet come into being, but it is through her every individual comes to life.

Aphrodite, Venus or Freyja is therefore not a pubescent woman, but a very weaned young girl, about seven years old, who in fact represents a fetus.

The word virgin comes from the common Indo-European * *varg: "vigor"*, like Sanskrit *ūrg: "force"*, *ūrga-jami: "to feed"*, like Greek ὀργάω, *orgaô: to swell,* ὀργή, *orgê: "impulse", "momentum"*.

The virgin, then, is the strength, the vigor, who is nourished and swells, grows, then the one who *takes her momentum*. Nothing to do with the modern definition, isn't it ? And yet, the etymological definition is indeed the exact definition, and undoubtedly the historically correct definition.

The fetuses are fed (but not by the mouth, hence the frequent notion of fasting, but paradoxically also of orgy) with blood. Only blood. The fetuses, as can be seen in very young premature babies, are very red from the third month (before they are considered embryos, and they are rather beige).

Obviously our ancestors knew this, as premature miscarriages and births also existed at the time. We even found one (or two?) Neanderthal fetal tomb(s) (*La Ferrassie 5* in France and possibly *Mezmaiskaya* in Russia), which is exceptional since such small bones generally disappear very quickly.

This is very well known today. Regardless of their genetic skin color, all premature babies are of a dark red color. This is due to the fact that their skin is so thin that it is almost transparent and lets us see the blood vessels.

This is why the little Red Riding Hood is red, this is why the child of the goddess Kumari of Nepal is fully dressed in red, this is why she is symbolically nourished with blood (during the *Inda Jatra festival*). It is also why she shouldn't touch the ground (she would be born) and is therefore carried during her rare excursions (like a fetus), or why she can't bleed (she would die or would be born). Are you wondering what Kumari means? *Virgin*, in Nepalese ...

And yet, it is not a young pubescent woman, but a *weaned* little girl often chosen today between two and seven years. It is replaced by another Kumari when it bleeds or, in practice, during its first menstruation. Some sources claim that it should be chosen at the time of the fall of her first tooth of milk, and that during her puberty she becomes human again. In practice these details are not all respected. (Cf *From Goddess to Mortal* written by the former Kumari Rashmila Shakya)

These traditions are probably so old that they go back to our common ancestor, the Neanderthal man. They have undoubtedly been kept longer in this remote and isolated region of Nepal, and today we can have access to them to understand them by comparing them to our European versions.

The Kumari is chosen in the Shakya caste, of Buddhist religion. It was traditionally the caste of the gold smiths (in Europe it will be among the symbolic dwarves). In fact, several are chosen. Several Shakya girls, weaned, from about two to seven years old. Their horoscope must correspond to that of the king, who is... Hindu.

Indeed, the Kumari is venerated both by Buddhists and Hindus, in this valley where these two religions have always cohabited. But that's not all. Small Kumaris must pass some kind of test or entrance ritual. The exact content of this test is kept secret, but some parts have been told, and it is here these traditions have their interest. The girls (two to seven years) are placed in a room, alone, with living lights. Around them, men disguised as demons are dancing and scaring them, and heads of freshly decapitated animals are brandished in front of them.

If the little girl screams or cries, she is brought to the outside. If she is calm, she is chosen as a new Kumari. Ian McDonald's story *The Little Goddess* describes very well what is happening, and the future Kumari explains that she was not afraid because she understood that they were masked men, not real demons, so that the chosen girl instinctively has a different way of seeing things, **as if she already knew them.**

Thus begins the news of Ian Mc Donald:

I remember the night I became a goddess.

The men collected me from the hotel at sunset. I was light-headed with hunger, for the child-assessors said I must not eat on the day of the test.

There were two other girls for the test staying in the same hotel. I did not know them; they were from other villages where the devi could live. Their parents wept unashamedly. I could not understand it; their daughters might be goddesses.

94

(…)

The room smelled of brassy metal. I did not recognize it then but I know it now as the smell of blood. Beneath the blood was another smell, of time piled thick as dust. One of the two women who would be my guardians if I passed the test told me the temple was five hundred years old. She was a short, round woman with a face that always seemed to be smiling, but when you looked closely you saw it was not. She made us sit on the floor on red cushions while the men brought the rest of the girls.

Some of them were crying already. When there were ten of us the two women left and the door was closed. We sat for a long time in the heat of the long room. Some of the girls fidgeted and chattered but I gave all my attention to the wall carvings and soon I was lost. It has always been easy for me to lose myself; in Shakya I could disappear for hours in the movement of clouds across the mountain, in the ripple of the grey river far below, and the flap of the prayer banner in the wind. My parents saw it as a sign of my inborn divinity, one of the thirty-two that mark those girls in whom the goddess may dwell.

In the failing light I read the story of Jayaprakash Malla playing dice with the devi Taleju Bhawani who came to him in the shape of a red snake and left with the vow that she would only return to the Kings of Kathmandu as a virgin girl of low caste, to spite their haughtiness. I could not read its end in the darkness, but I did not need to. I was its end, or one of the other nine low-caste girls in the god-house of the devi.

Then the doors burst open wide and firecrackers exploded and through the rattle and smoke red demons leaped into the hall. Behind them men in crimson beat pans and clappers and bells. At once two of the girls began to cry and the two women came and took them away. But I knew the monsters were just silly men. In masks. These were not even close to demons. I have seen demons, after the rain clouds when the light comes low down the valley and all the mountains leap up as one. Stone demons, kilometers high. I have heard their voices, and their breath does not smell like onions. The silly men danced close to me, shaking their red manes and red tongues, but I could see their eyes behind the painted holes and they were afraid of me.

Then the door banged open again with another crash of fireworks and more men came through the smoke. They carried baskets draped with red sheets. They set them in front of us and whipped away the coverings. Buffalo heads, so freshly struck off the blood was bright and glossy. Eyes rolled up, lolling tongues still warm, noses still wet. And the flies, swarming around the severed neck. A man pushed a basket towards me on my cushion as if it were a dish of holy food. The crashing and beating outside rose to a roar, so loud and metallic it hurt. The girl from my own Shakya village started to wail; the cry spread to another and then another, then a fourth.

The other woman, the tall pinched one with a skin like an old purse, came in to take them out, carefully lifting her gown so as not to trail it in the blood. The dancers whirled around like flame and the kneeling man lifted the buffalo head from the basket.

He held it up in my face, eye to eye, but all I thought was that it must weigh a lot; his muscles stood out like vines, his arm shook. The flies looked like black jewels. Then there was a clap from outside and the men set down the heads and covered them up with their cloths and they left with the silly demon men whirling and leaping around them.

There was one other girl left on her cushion now. I did not know her. She was of a Vajryana family from Niwar down the valley. We sat a long time, wanting to talk but not knowing if silence was part of the trial. Then the door opened a third time and two men led a white goat into the devi hall. They brought it right between me and the Niwari girl. I saw its wicked, slotted eye roll. One held the goat's tether, the other took a big ceremonial kukri from a leather sheath. He blessed it and with one fast strong stroke sent the goat's head leaping from its body.

I almost laughed, for the goat looked so funny, its body not knowing where its head was, the head looking around for the body and then the body realizing that it had no head and going down with a kick, and why was the Niwari girl screaming, couldn't she see how funny it was, or was she screaming because I saw the joke and she was jealous of that? Whatever her reason, smiling woman and weathered woman came and took her very gently away and the two men went down on their knees in the spreading blood and kissed the wooden floor.

They lifted away the two parts of the goat. I wished they hadn't done that. I would have liked someone with me in the big wooden hall. But I was on my own in the heat and the dark and then, over the traffic, I heard the deep-voiced bells of Kathmandu start to swing and ring. For the last time the doors opened and there were the women, in the light.

"Why have you left me all alone?" I cried. "What have I done wrong?"

"How could you do anything wrong, goddess?" said the old, wrinkled woman who, with her colleague, would become my mother and father and teacher and sister. "Now come along with us and hurry. The King is waiting."

"Your home, goddess,"

Outside this palace you shall not touch the ground. The moment you touch the ground, you cease to be divine.

You will wear red, with your hair in a topknot and your toe- and fingernails painted. You will carry the red tilak of Siva on your forehead. We will help you with your preparations until they become second nature.

You will speak only within the confines of your palace, and little even then. Silence becomes the Kumari. You will not smile or show any emotion.

You will not bleed. Not a scrape, not a scratch. The power is in the blood and when the blood leaves, the devi leaves. On the day of your first blood, even one single drop, we will tell the priest and he will inform the King that the goddess has left. You will no longer be divine and you will leave this palace and return to your family. You will not bleed.

You have no name. You are Taleju, you are Kumari. You are the goddess.

The little Kumari is chosen as the small human in which the goddess Taleju is reincarnated. This goddess is reincarnated only in a little pre-pubescent girl, and it is she who gives the king her power. Without Kumari, the Hindu king of Nepal has no power, or, I prefer to say so now, *no life*. Without Kumari (the virgin, the fetus), he is not alive. The Kumari actually represents *his own life*. Every year at *the Indra Jatra festival*, the king must renew his power. Does this mean that this tradition was common in Europe? It is quite possible ... For this, he visits the Kumari, who puts a crown flower (avatar of the umbilical cord: rebirth) around the neck, and he gives her a gold piece (treasure) in exchange.

As I have explained above, let us say again that this little goddess is always dressed in red and gold (blood and light), with a red cap on her head (the amniotic bag, the hat) and the third eye, red, on the forehead. She wears different jewelry, and one of them, the most important, is a snake-shaped necklace (the umbilical cord).

She must never touch the ground, and many women come to see her for problems related to fertility and female cycles that they hope to see healing. The festival of Indra Jatra lasts in 8 days. It starts by erecting a tree trunk in the city (the umbilical cord, the placenta) and then follows various procession. The Kumari is carried, always in a chariot, and there will be sacrificed many animals for her because she will symbolically be nourished by blood. At the end of the festival, the tree is cut down (symbol of birth: the cord is cut).

The lifting of the Yosin pole in Katmandhou during the festival of Indra Jatra.

It is clear that the Kumari represents the fetus, life.

In the *Enquête sur les Kumaris* published by Niloufar Moaven, it is noted that two of the 32 signs of recognition of a future Kumari are as follows:

5. *Janlangulihasta padata: feet and hands like a duck*

21. *Brahmasvara kalividkaruta svarata: grave voice like that of a sparrow*.

Two of these signs are *a priori* "wacky" but are related to birds, as... the descriptions related to our princesses in Europe (often they even sing like birds), because these traditions have in fact the same origin. Again the gender of these symbols doesn't have the meaning that is given to it today. These are symbols.

Of course the fetus is symbolically feminine (and consequently also the child up to seven years old, because these sexual characteristics are not very developed), since its gender is unknown and since it stays in an unquestionably feminine environment, in the very essence of femininity.

Thus the virgin, the female fetus is often mixed with the symbolism of the mother who gives herself life. In fact, we will describe it later, the fetus, then the baby, and even the child until weaning (physiologically seven years), *is not an individual* (it is not a divisible being), so it is not really *a person*. That is why in traditions, the world is created in seven days: it is always the world seen through individual eyes. Let us remember that mythology is an *individual, subjective* and not objective path as is usually believed.

CHAPTER THREE
The Fire Bull

At the beginning of the second symbolic pregnancy (the one that begins at Easter, when the first one ends), the fetus grows at the same time as the sun. At the summer solstice on June 21, about two and a half months since the onset of pregnancy, three months of amenorrhoea, according to the modern calculation method (three months since the last menstruation).

If Easter is placed late, at least two months, or eight weeks (or ten weeks of amenorrhoea) are obtained. This date is very interesting, because it is from these eight weeks that the future baby is called fetus rather than embryo. The difference lies in a simple thing: it has all its internal organs, and therefore it is "human." There is another thing: as explained above, it is between these two dates that the proportion of miscarriages (linked to nonviable embryos) decreases and then disappears. After 10 weeks of pregnancy (12 weeks of amenorrhea), spontaneous miscarriages related to nonviable embryos are non-existent.

Note that Easter was probably originally placed around March 21, at the spring equinox, exactly three months before the summer solstice.

The pregnancy is then celebrated and externalized. Even today it is usual not to declare a pregnancy before that date, because before, it is potentially unsustainable. Thus official, the fetus with human form is shown, it is *illuminated.*

Similarly, there is an analogy between this change and the change between childhood and the age of individuality (from the age of seven). So the bonfire on summer solstice is a way to burn childhood years, as the baby teeth that are leaving.

We are now in summer, and at this moment we must speak of another symbol. The bull, and the cow. The bull is all the representations of the bull that we know, in myths, in traditions, everywhere. It is the minotaur, it is the centaur (which is not originally a horse but a bull, hence its name cen-*taure*), it is the bulls and the cows of the painted caves, it is also the bull of the Chauvet cave, the one that is intertwined with a lioness, it is the cult of Mithra, it is the myth of Atlantis, it is the primitive cow Auðhumbla of Norse mythology, it is the sacred cows in India, it is Apis in Egyptian mythology, it is modern bullfighting, and it is probably even the reason why we still drink cow's milk.

Why has no one seen the evidence? The cow has an exactly identical gestation period to that of the woman. There is no clearer symbol. 280 days (40 weeks) for the cow, 280 days (40 weeks) for European women, 270 days (or about 39 weeks) for the world average. It is the only animal that has an identical gestation period. (See for example: *Does gestation vary by ethnic group? A London-based study of over 122,000 pregnancies with spontaneous onset of labour* par Roshni R Patel et al., 2004).

But there is more. In the wild world (this is still the case with some domestic cows), European animals have a period of anestrus and a period of estrus in the year. In other words, a period of fertility and a period of infertility.

This is so because the births come at the most favorable season for the survival of the young, whereas winter could be fatal (lack of food, but especially the predators who could easily hunt in the snow). For cattle, this birth should ideally be in the spring. In fact, males and females mate nine months before, during the summer (July-August). As everyone knows, naturally the bulls fight to be able to mate and bullfights are among the most violent in animals. The bulls symbolically have the strength of the sun, since it is also in summer that the sun is the strongest: this is among others why Apis and other sacred cattle are represented with the sun between the horns. The bull is an avatar of the sun, but not only...

It is also an avatar of the fetus, at the precise moment when it begins to be felt. Indeed, at around four months of pregnancy, the movements of the fetus are identifiable for the mother. In other words, the fetus begins to strike, it begins to fight. This battle has several aims: to be chosen, as we shall see later, therefore, like the bull, to fight with the rival; but also, to get out. Get out of the womb, and get out of the grave.

Well, that's not all; in fact, it goes further: the bull is what we would have called today the spermatozoon, and the sun between the horns the ovule. The bull caught the sun, or the sun caught the bull.

We'll stop a little, and I'll give you some evidence...

One of the other signs of recognition of a Kumari is the following (*Enquête sur les Kumaris*, by Niloufar Moaven):

23. Gopadma netrata: eyelashes like those of a cow (others translate as "a heifer")

About the cult of Apis, it must be remembered that he is associated with the god Re, and is represented carrying the solar disk between his horns. When he died, the bull Apis was the avatar of the god Osiris and was then bound to funeral traditions. He was sometimes represented as a bull, bringing the body of the deceased to his tomb, carrying it on his back.

The mother of the bull who is representing the god Apis was also sacred and venerated. According to legend, he had been fertilized by a lightning: the sun and light in other words.

The cult of Apis was taken up again in the Greco-Roman tradition, in the form of the god Serapis.

Statue of the bull Apis found in Rome

This is the mother and son who are revered (the pregnant woman, the pregnant cow). But that's not all. When the bull god dies, it is necessary to choose a new bull. This one was generally a year old (at weaning: the calf being then an individual, and thus his personality is recognizable by the others, so to speak). When he was chosen, a stable was built for him, oriented towards the east, in which he had to remain and be fed, by priests only, for forty days.

After that, he was escorted by one hundred priests (10, like 10 months or 280 days: 28x10) to the Nilopolis temple. He remained there four months, during which he received the visit of all the women who wished. They were then given a pledge of fertility.

After these four months, Apis left the city of Nilopolis, escorted by the hundred priests, to go to Memphis down the Nile (following the water is a symbol of pregnancy and birth).

Let us now turn to the myth of Atlantis in *the Critias* of Plato (translation by Emile Chambry):

As to offices and honours, the following was the arrangement from the first. Each of the ten kings in his own division and in his own city had the absolute control of the citizens, and, in most cases, of the laws, punishing and slaying whomsoever he would. Now the order of precedence among them and their mutual relations were regulated by the commands of Poseidon which the law had handed down. These were inscribed by the first kings on a pillar of orichalcum, which was situated in the middle of the island, at the temple of Poseidon, whither the kings were gathered together every fifth and every sixth year alternately, thus giving equal honour to the odd and to the even number. And when they were gathered together they consulted about their common interests, and enquired if any one had transgressed in anything and passed judgment and before they passed judgment they gave their pledges to one another on this wise:

- There were bulls who had the range of the temple of Poseidon; and the ten kings, being left alone in the temple, after they had offered prayers to the god that they might capture the victim which was acceptable to him, hunted the bulls, without weapons but with staves and nooses; and the bull which they caught they led up to the pillar and cut its throat over the top of it so that the blood fell upon the sacred inscription. Now on the pillar, besides the laws, there was inscribed an oath invoking mighty curses on the disobedient. **When therefore, after slaying the bull in the accustomed manner, they had burnt its limbs, they filled a bowl of wine and cast in a clot of blood for each of them; the rest of the victim they put in the fire, after having purified the column all round. Then they drew from the bowl in golden cups and pouring a libation on the fire, they swore that they would judge according to the laws on the pillar,** and would punish him who in any point had already transgressed them, and that for the future they would not, if they could help, offend against the writing on the pillar, and would neither command others, nor obey any ruler who commanded them, to act otherwise than according to the laws of their father Poseidon. This was the prayer which each of them offered up for himself and for his descendants, at the same time drinking and dedicating the cup out of which he drank in the temple of the god; and after they had supped and satisfied their needs, when darkness came on, and the fire about the sacrifice was cool, all of them put on most beautiful azure robes, and, sitting on the ground, at night, over the embers of the sacrifices by which they had sworn, and extinguishing all the fire about the temple, they

received and gave judgment, if any of them had an accusation to bring against any one; and when they given judgment, at daybreak they wrote down their sentences on a golden tablet, and dedicated it together with their robes to be a memorial.

I will speak more of the myth of Atlantis, but this description, which can be brought closer to the cult of Mithra, is interesting. The cult of Mithra was practiced in ancient times in temples (*mithræum, mithræa*). Originally, these are natural caves, and later artificial caves: they are narrow and without light, probably much like the temple in which the test of the new Kumari takes place.

These temples are very interesting to describe in relation to our research. They are divided into three parts:

The antechamber; **The spelæum or spelunca** (the cave), a large room decorated with paintings in which sacred meals take place; **The sanctuary**, at the bottom of the cave, in which the altar and the image, *the image is in the form of a painting, a sculpture or a statue, of Mithra giving death to the bull.*

Mithras sacrificing the bull

There is no direct testimony, of course, because the Mithra's cult tells of a too intimate, too miniature event so that we can in fact not understand how it was explained with such precision at a time when did not even know microscopes.

Remember that the world must always be perceived individually in myths.

I will tell you the story of Mithra in another way, with more modern words:

Mithra was born, near a placenta (sacred tree) and the amniotic bag (sacred spring), he has a cap (the amniotic bag). Two elements are nested in each other. There's no time, remember.

The primordial bull is the father (the spermatozoids move with the vigor of bulls), Mithra is, somehow, at this stage, the egg. The egg catches the bull (interesting version of fertilization...): the spermatozoa, you will have understood (he is caught by the horns, the head ...), and takes him into the cave, that means the uterus.

In the uterus, a raven, the messenger of the gods, the mother, *the hormones*, explains to Mithra, the egg-fetus, that he has to sacrifice the spermatozoa. Indeed, this one is impaled (he is fixed with the umbilical cord) to become a source of life. He will nourish and then help the fetus, with this transformed wheat (the mother's food), and that blood-wine. The animals from the semen collected by the moon are the image of the male part of the fetus, the mortal part, collected by the moon, that is to say, an avatar of the egg.

Mithra, etymologically speaking, means "friend", "ally", ally yes, that is to say "the one who is bound", "the one who is attached" (by the umbilical cord).

In fact, when we say "Mithra is born," he is not "born" in the present sense, he is simply conceived. Conceived close to the sacred stone (the heart of the mother, the stone always indicating the heart, and it is called *"Petra generatrix"* and it is in fact she who is at the origin of this life. It is the famous philosopher's stone too, but... it can also refer to the ovary), the sacred tree (the Placenta), the sacred source (the amniotic fluid).

In Mithraism there are several stages of initiation. Seven. In fact seven years. We'll talk about that later.

The seventh of the twelve works of Heracles is to subdue the Cretan bull of Minos, which he had not agreed to return to Poseidon. That is to say, in the seventh month of the year (July), he must subdue the Cretan bull of Minos. Yes, because Heracles is indeed our seven-year-old child, who passes the year of the three symbolic pregnancies before becoming "himself", "the ancestor."

The plan of the cave of Lascaux is almost that of a *mithraeum*, in any case concerning the great chamber and the sanctuary (here called *"the Well"*). You will agree, it is at least strange. But stranger still, this impression is repeated in several ornate prehistoric caves.

There is no doubt that no one wants to see analogies in this, for they refuse to link so distant periods, and yet the caves reveal the same man-bird several times (In France in *Combarelles*, and *Pech-Merle*: the so-called "man wounded man" has what I call a bird above his head...), and the same bull (or bison)-man (or bison) (In France: *Les Trois Frères*, *Chauvet*...). The bull-bison and the cow are ubiquitous in the parietal representations (whereas the man hunted mainly reindeer), especially in *Lascaux*.

The sacrificed bull, and *Mithra* is thus also this image:

"The Well", painting of the Lascaux cave
(-17,000 years, Montignac, France)

The Sorcerer from Gabillou, France.

Man-bull chimeras are common in ornate caves. In the Chauvet cave in France, a man-bull seems to mate with a lioness-woman, these two chimeras are painted on a stone stalactite in the form of male genetalia.

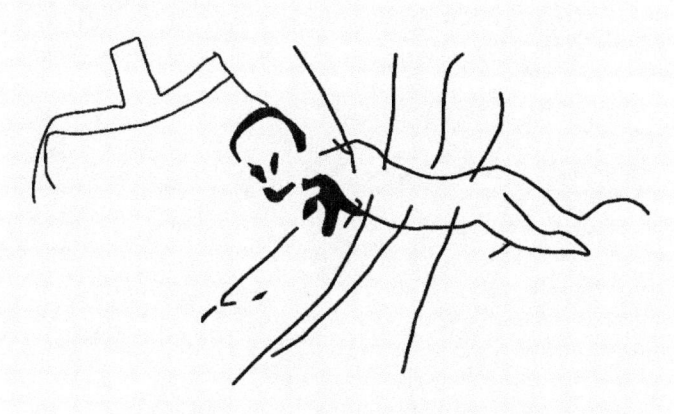

Reproduction of the wounded man, Pech-Merle, France

For me, it is called "the man and the bird", indeed it seems to me to see a bird above his head and not "a tective sign" or "sign of type Placard" as it was described .

There is an almost identical painting in the cave of Cougnac (France, Lot, 50km from Pech-Merle).

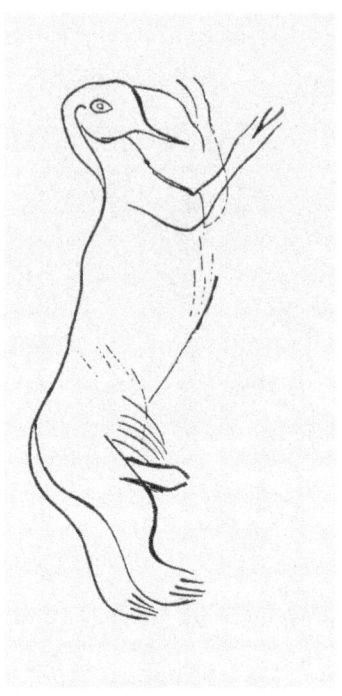

Another man-bird chimera, Altamira, Spain

Keep in mind these man-bird or man-bull chimeras, with a clearly drawn genetalia, they will be useful to understand the very end of this work.

In fact, there is an important analogy between bullfighting in summer (for breeding), and the "fighting" between the egg and the spermatozoon, and the baby who is beginning "to move" according to the modern expression or "to fight" according to the probable ancient expression. We must of course understand that the cave, in the tradition of *Mithraism* in particular, is *the belly, the uterus.*

The sacrificed one is the imaginary enemy: the other bull, the adversary. The other bull, the adversary? It is like the baby spent all the pregnancy trying to be chosen, to win the fight. If he is born dead, or if there is a miscarriage, then he is defeated, if he is born healthy, then he has won. Like the bull who fights to be chosen, and finally be able to obtain a descent, the spermatozoon fights, and the ancestor fights to enter his new body, so that this new body can be born and come out of the grave: the three images are identical.

The sacrificed bull is therefore the adversary, but in fact, if we look carefully, the bulls often fight and are replaced *when they are too old*. So when they are too old, they are put to death *by the youngest*, often it is even the son who fights with the father. Whoever won, "the king of the bulls", if one may say, is just one of the new generation; The adversary is indeed the ancestor himself, once again. In a way, then, the child fights against the ancestor. He fights against himself. He is put to death by himself, in order to be chosen: to be reborn. Like Óðinn hanging in the sacrificial tree: *himself given to himself.*

In this sense, the spilled blood is what nourishes him, the little piece of life that remains gives the necessary spark for the beginning of his new body, if I can express it in its modern words. Like the tree that produces a tiny seed, with a tiny dose of energy, the quintessence of itself, so that it can begin to live (again), and *eat the world around it*.

Let us not forget that the fetus feeds on blood, whose avatar in all ancient myths is wine.

Alcohol in general, produced by the fermentation of food, is an image of the products of the interior of the body; In other words transformed and fermented by the organism. The killing of the bull is not negative, it is simply the symbol of its reincarnation, and it is indeed this one that makes it possible.

The fetus therefore fights with the ancestor, from the fourth or fifth month of pregnancy, or, for this second symbolic pregnancy, in summer, like bulls. Pregnancy is a battle, a war. We can now understand the traditions of bullfighting, where the man-fetus-young child fights with the ancestor-bull to put him to death, or to put *himself* (the elder himself) to death, and thus be reborn.

Similarly, the minotaur is put to death by Theseus and helped by Ariane (the girl: life, mother), it emerges from the labyrinth (the womb) thanks to the thread given by her (the cordon umbilical). The bull: the spermatozoon, is killed by Mithra: the egg, and is used to feed it. In other words, the ancestor bull is put to death by the child-ancestor, to nourish it (it becomes the placenta, an image all the more troubling when it is known that the placenta is created with the genes of the father) but it is not him who consumes or eats himself directly. Symbolically. To understand who eats the ancestor-bull, we must look again at Nature.

CHAPTER FOUR
The Bloody Lioness

In Nature, the animal that kills and devours bulls is, for example, the lioness. The lioness is the symbol of the carnivore. It puts to death quickly and efficiently, swallows up 30 kg of meat at once, and her mouth is so stained with blood. The lioness or the lion, but rather the lioness. It should be remembered that these were present in Europe (cave lions), they were even represented in caves (*Chauvet Pont d'Arc* cave in France for example). The lioness consumes meat, to feed the lion cubs, *the descendants, the children.* In short, the lioness is a kind of "placenta", a sort of buffer between death and life.

In fact, the lioness is the other side of the placenta, *the devouring side*, which is stained with blood, the maternal side. That is what she represents, everywhere. And the same for the well-known sphinx, which is usually female.

*Reproduction of the lionesses from
the Cave of Chauvet Pont d'Arc
(France, -35,000 years old)*

You're not convinced? So let us look at the etymology of the word sphinx: From ancient Greek Σφίγξ, *Sphí(n)gx*, and from Sanskrit स्थग *sthag*, means "concealed" or "hidden".

Concealed? Why if not the placenta? The sphinxes are not concealed... Unless... It is indeed the reason why the etymology of this word is not understood today.

The lion, the cat, is the attribute of the witch (the midwife); it is also the attribute of Freyja (the virgin, the egg, the fetus), which has two of them, which she uses to draw her chariot: the placenta).

They are big cats, lynxes, in other words very quiet and discreet predators. Here we have another explanation for this symbol: the "devouring maternal side" is replaced by felines because not only is it an unrivaled predator, but it is also very discreet and silent, invisible, so to speak, like the placenta.

There are also lioness goddesses. Sometimes the lioness goddesses have a mane, like the male lions. In fact this is not surprising as they are humanized, and this mane becomes the hair. Precisely. The other side of the placenta (the fetal side) is often represented, in the tales and mythology, by a tree, a snake or dragon, or hair, among other things. These are the hair of Medusa, before magnificent, then transformed into snakes. These are also the hair of Rapunzel. But we'll come back to that.

Then there are two images of this same side of the placenta: the devourer, and the nourishing mother. We have the example in Egyptian mythology with the goddess Sekhmet: a lioness, and her other version, the cat goddess Bastet. You will see that this placenta-lion feeds on blood and is eager for it:

The lion-man is a figure present in Mithraism. Like the caduceus, he has two serpents intertwined around him (the umbilical cord with the vein and/or the two arteries).

Remember the keys in the hands.

Sekhmet and Pharaoh

It is said about Sekhmet, that to prevent her from killing all humans, Rê had to prepare a drink of beer colored in red (like wine, an avatar of the blood, but of course, in the absence of wine, they colored the beer!). So appeased, she turns into Hathor, the goddess of fertility.

Strange that this bloody goddess is replaced by the goddess of fertility, right? But if it represents the placenta then everything is explained.

Hathor in the form of a cow.

Hathor, who is a cow, is one of the most important goddesses of ancient Egypt. She is the nurse of Pharaoh, but also "the mistress of the West" who welcomes the dead for their journey to their new life. It also helps women to give birth and is the patroness of minors. Strange mixture? Or?

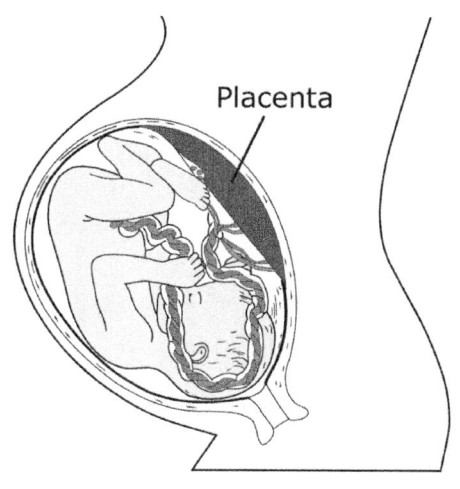

Placenta in the uterus

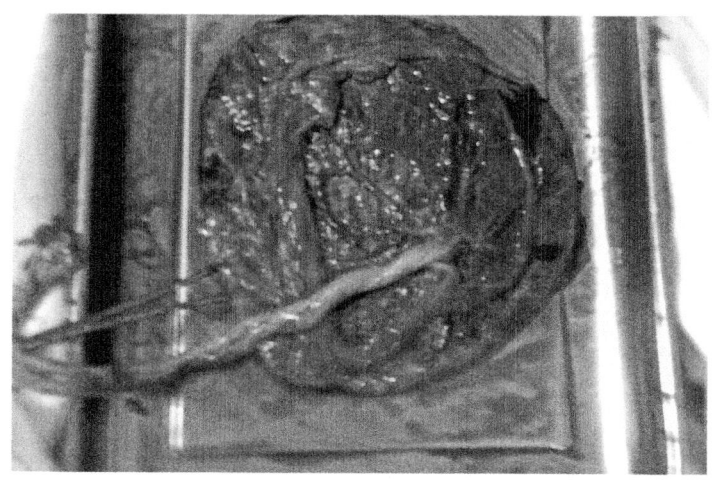

Human placenta, fetal side, with the "branching pattern"

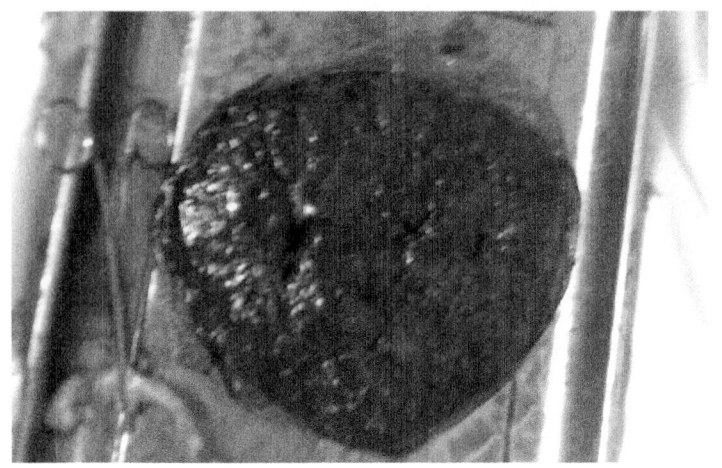

Human placenta, maternal side

Everything here is interesting. Concerning minors, and keys, you will understand later. For the rest, here is my explanation: Sekhmet-Hathor is *responsible for the death of men* (understand: the death of ancestors), for she is the one who can give them life (or not). In order to give life, Sekhmet-Hathor must be nourished with blood, of course a little transformed blood: the famous beer colored in red. At the moment when she is fed with blood, the massacre ceases, that is to say, life begins: she turns into Hathor, the goddess of fertility and birth, for she can then give life. Of course she welcomes the dead in their new life and she is "mistress of the West" (of the kingdom of the dead, the West representing the death of the sun), because we are talking about, I repeat, a rebirth : she gives life back to the ancestor.

Bastet, the cat goddess, is *the nourishing side* of the placenta, or the fetal side (when Sekhmet the lioness is *the devouring side*, or the maternal side):

Bastet is a face of Sekhmet. She is the daughter of Ra or Amon. When she is in the shape of a cat, she is the benevolent protector of humanity, she is the goddess of music, joy, and the goddess of childbirth. Often she is represented with a smile on her lips. However, when she becomes angry, she is then identified with Sekhmet, the goddess of war. She is attractive and dangerous, sweet and cruel.

Her attractive goddess-cat side has the power to stimulate love (like the placenta which probably plays a role in the secretion of oxytocin: the hormone of love and attachment and the trigger of childbirth) and protects women and children. Bastet is the symbol of femininity and maternity, and the protector of home. She fights the serpent Apophis, or Seth. Bastet is the wife of Atoum and she gave birth to the lion Miysis (Greek Mihos).

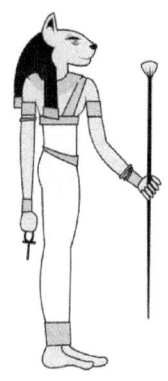

In a tomb of the valley of the Queens, she is represented with knives to protect Pharaoh, whom she is supposed to have birthed and nursed. Bastet is "on the other side": she cuts (with her attribute the knife) the umbilical cord (Apophis or Apep) to help the unborn child (*Ra to revive*: remember, life is only possible only through the energy of the sun, which is like "slowed down" in it).

The goddess Bastet

Apophis is a gigantic serpent (the umbilical cord), the enemy of Ra. He is considered a god of night, the personification of chaos, he seeks to destroy the divine creation. Apophis swallows the water (the amniotic fluid) that surrounds the solar boat (the newborn) to prevent its rebirth every day. However, he is defeated every time by Bastet, the cat of Ra, slaughtered and beheaded with a knife (after birth). This is explained in the Book of the Dead (in my opinion, a manual to the child for the ancestor reincarnation in himself).

In some scenes in temples, the king or pharaoh during the battle is represented with a round object that symbolizes the eye of Apophis (the navel, of course). The myth of Apophis is often explained by concerns posed by solar eclipses. You understand that I don't believe in that explanation. The analysis of mythologies must always be *individual*. The sun is the sun or light visible at birth, life is sometimes compromised at birth, as the serpent Apophis, the umbilical cord, wanted to keep the child hooked to him in the darkness of the womb. To live fully, one must succeed in detaching from him. Apophis is sometimes depicted as coming out of a tree (the placenta).

When we are thinking about cat and lion in ancient Egypt, we must think especially about the great Sphinx of Giza.

And precisely... we know from the traces on his face and from the writings of Pliny the Elder that he was originally covered with red painted plaster, in other words, the color of the blood, like the stained mouth of the lioness, like the maternal side of the placenta, which, in fact *eats* the mother: *devours her flesh* in her womb and literally *drinks her blood* to nourish the fetus.

It is interesting to dwell on the fact that the pharaoh or the king is represented with a round object representing the eye of Apophis as if he had kept something from him. Of course, it is the famous third eye, belonging to him, to the kingdom of the dead and the fetus, that which has been detached from the head of the serpent: in other words it is also the navel, the mark of the bite of the snake. It is actually the third eye in the middle of the forehead on the head of the serpent (which is also the ancestor, and therefore the pharaoh or the reincarnated himself), and the navel on the belly of the newborn, *the new body*.

There are other elements: the "real" chimera, for example, is a legendary animal composed of a lion's body (placenta on *the maternal side*) and a snake-shaped tail (placenta on *the fetal side*), with the head of a goat in the middle of the body.

A chimera

The two extremes (lion and snake) have now been explained. The goat, or the sheep, is the avatar of the god Pan, the name Pan means "Everything". The god Pan, god of music and the flute of Pan, represents, like his symbol the goat, I think, energy, life flowing, blood, *the matter in action*, so to speak.

Music, as we shall see later, represents exactly that. The goat in the middle is the symbol of vital energy, blood, life flowing.

That is why the shepherd is the symbol of the ancestor. With his bent stick or his shepherd's hook (also possessed by death, by the way) he catches the sheep or the goat, or rather the kid or lamb (think about Easter), that is to say he catches the child in who he is going to live again in, he catches *life (so... that is what the death is catching with that stick... life)*.

Of course, this shepherd cane is itself an avatar of the umbilical cord which, literally, *catches the fetus*.

You should know that the symbol of the lion is not from Egypt, but it can be found much earlier. It is a very present symbol in prehistory, both in artifacts and in decorated caves.

The problem of symbolic analyzes related to these prehistoric artifacts or paintings is that they are biased. Archaeologists often look at these artifacts with their psychology. They see what they want to see in relation to what they believe these humans were, without first telling themselves that they perhaps don't know. I caricature a little, but unfortunately it is often the case.

As they saw statuettes of plump or even fat women, they said "here is the female ideal of prehistory" and "this is created because they hoped that their wives would be fertile" or the so classical *"this is a goddess of fertility"*. It's really ridiculous. This is a personal psychological analysis without any foundation or logic. They don't really look at the statues and they are so locked in their books that they have no experience of life. Did our ancestors really have fertility problems?

In fact, these statues clearly represent, objectively, women who have just given birth. They are fat, probably in an exaggerated way, but in fact because getting fat was a good thing during pregnancy. The breasts are swollen, as they are a few days after childbirth because they are filled with milk.

Finally, the belly is large but flaccid, as it is after a childbirth, because the uterus, empty, has not yet retracted to regain its size outside pregnancy.

This is not the feminine ideal but the woman who has given birth *and is alive*, which was probably less frequent than today. It is a female state. The state of nurturing mother. The one that gives and maintains life, like Mother Earth.

The lion man (Löwenmensch), ivory sculpture Cave of Hohlenstein, Germany, -32,000 years

I wanted to talk about this in order to introduce *"the lion-man"* (Germany, 32,000 years old), which, in my opinion, is not a man. Archaeologists see a human being without prominent breasts or clear female forms, so they call him *"a man"*. Actually, I think it's a girl. The triangular shape of the pubis is probably characteristic of a feminine pubis, and the lion's head is rather that of a lioness. But this is not so important.

I recently saw that the authors of her reconstitution think it is a female, so things can change, the points of view too. In any case, here is our *first sphinx*. He should have been called that way.

The sphinx, the concealed.

*Note the **seven** horizontal lines engraved on the left arm.*

Another sphinx, perhaps more clear, is that of the *Chauvet cave (France, -35,000)*, in addition to the magnificent lionesses represented there, there is this very clear image: *a female body surmounted by a head of a lioness entwined by a male body surmounted by a bull's head.* The ancestor who embraces and takes possession of the body of the lioness, for that is what he does, paradoxically, when *eaten*, we become what we eat, remember that. We find the same symbolism as in the cult of Mithra. Mithra is the lioness, the egg, the bull, the spermatozoon, eaten by the egg. The belly of the lioness in this cave is... enormous. This relationship between what is eaten and pregnancy (which are, in fact, both *"what is in the belly"*) is striking in many traditions and tales, where, for example, we are covered with an animal fur (we become the animal or we are *in the animal*) and tales such as, of course, Little Red Riding Hood or the wolf Fenrir who swallows the god Óðinn in Norse mythology.

Finally, in *Investigation about Kumaris (enquête sur les Kumaris)* published by Niloufar Moaven, we find that other sign, that is, with the signs mentioned above concerning birds and cows, and the last that will be soon, the only signs relating to animals:

15. Simha hanuta : les joues comme un lion (cheeks like a lion)

Well, let us return to our story, you will soon know what is happening in these caves, and you'll know why Hathor is also the patroness of miners, but one thing at a time... The bull fights take place in summer, and the lioness-placenta consumes the dead bull, *that is to say the dead ancestor,* to give away his blood, and thus feed the fetus, *that is to say the ancestor -child.* Of course, both lion and bull are related to the sun, since both are symbols of summer, so their vigor in combat is the same as the vigor of the sun in summer. Summer is also the number seven, as the seventh solar month of the year is July and the seventh day of the week is Sunday, like the seven years of the weaned child.

In this regard, in the story of Theseus, (who kills the Minotaur in the labyrinth, and then emerges from it with help from the cord - umbilical cord - given by Ariane) it is reported that he was raised with his maternal grandfather (also he is an orphan), and that he was very brave from childhood. In fact, when Heracles had stopped at the palace of Trezene and had thrown his lion-skin tunic on the ground, and when all the children fled frightened, the seven years old Theseus, rushed towards it with an ax.

You will see that the choice 'of the ax is not insignificant, even if other sources cite a sword (that is the same). Of course, the little Theseus attacks the skin to put it on himself and thus become the lion.

CHAPTER FIVE
Autumn, the Key and the Crown

As I told you before, a crown was given to the weaned child, king of the year. He has already used it, symbolically, for the combat he must lead as a fetus, in the womb, he who strikes to go out. For the child, the exit of the womb in this symbolic pregnancy is also the exit of the tomb for the ancestor.

Gundestrup Cauldron

On this piece of the Gundestrup cauldron we can distinguish one of the rare representations of the god Cernunnos (the god Pan), with his antlers (his crown), and holding a snake and a necklace or torque (an avatar of the snake-umbilical cord, but also here, with the torque, of the cervix), a deer, a goat, a lion, and probably a dog. The dog is responsible for providing the dead in *the afterlife*. Its notable flair but also its ability to see in the night make it a discrete, real and symbolic guide. He can see (smell) what we can not see.

Probably it was one of the first reasons for the domestication of the dog: it was *a flashlight*, so to speak, a guide. In myths, it always has this role.

Perhaps it was more important than that, perhaps he was able to smell the bones, the buried dead, and thus find the graves in the prehistoric rites of reincarnation. Perhaps it was used for these purposes. (Let's say it by the way: the use of cadaver dogs in archeology is beginning - again).

A dog or a wolf follows the footprints of the child in *the Chauvet cave* (France), the wolf-dog always arrives before (always eats first): it is he who indicates the way to *Little Red Riding Hood*, towards the tomb of his grandmother, he is the one who first eats corn in the *worship of Mithra*, it is *Anubis* in ancient Egypt. The wolf-dog is not only the guide of the new body towards the tomb, but it is also the one who guards the tomb during the reincarnation of the dead, that is why *he eats the food of the master*, in the myths, whereas this one can not do so.

Thus, he is the guard of the kingdom of the dead, in the myths, and, for example in Nordic mythology, the wolves of Óðinn Geri and Freki receive Óðinn's food while he is himself in Valhalla (the womb) and drinks only wine (blood). The totem of humans in Europe is par excellence the wolf, we will speak about that latter.

But what does all this mean?

The wolf-dog is, of course, an avatar of the mother (her belly), just like the bear, which is another image. The mother keeps the kingdom of the dead, and the kingdom of the dead, the grave, is also the uterus. Not only does she guide the dead to her, but she also protects them. Are you skeptical? Geri and Freki mean "voracious" and "hard", good qualifiers for the pregnant woman (or her belly), as for the wolf and the bear. But that's not all. They eat Óðinn's food while he only drinks wine (blood) while he is in Valhalla (in the womb). You understood. It is the mother who eats the food of the fetus while he only receives blood from her.

Let us continue with Norse mythology: The Fenrir wolf (Fenrir means *wet closed place*, the womb therefore) is attached by a cord, a thin ribbon named *Gleipnir*. This ribbon is attached to a pile or a stone embedded a little further. It is *the linea nigra*, a dark line that appears on the belly of three-quarters of pregnant women, and which seems to hang from their navel, starting from the pubis. Fenrir is tied, his face is the female genitals, bloodily red. The wolf roars and drool flows from its jaw (vaginal discharge and loss of amniotic liquid). He will deliver himself at *Ragnarök*, the great battle (which is none other than the birth: the end of the world of the gods at Valhalla), he will then have the mouth torn by Viðarr (as the frequent tearings of childbirth).

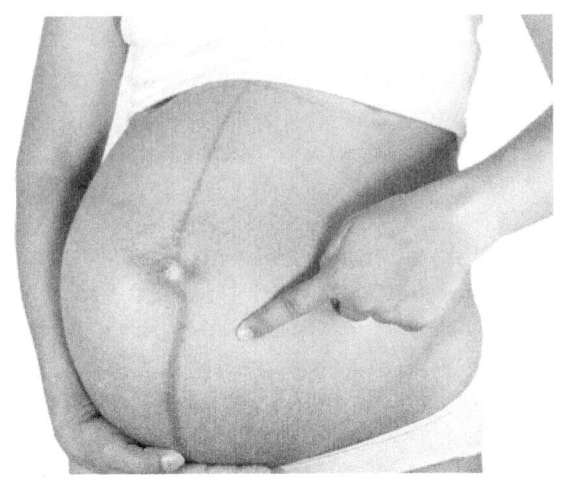

Linea nigra

The wolf Fenrir is Cerberus, the dog with three heads who guards the kingdom of the dead. It is also Garm, in Norse mythology, Garm means *"the devourer"*. It is also the famous *"domino mask" (in French it is called "the wolf")*, the classic little black mask that hides the eyes: it is the same. Three heads, or sometimes two, always represented side by side. *And yet, they are not side by side, but following each other* (it is the female sex: *labia majora or vulva, labia minora, cervix*): we must kill (cross) the three heads to reach the world of the dead. Very interesting about this is the story of Persephone (*the girl*), lost by her mother Demeter (*the mother, the she-wolf*).

The mother looks then for nine days and nine nights (*that means nine months pregnancy*) before learning by Hélios (*the sun*) that her daughter was abducted by Hades (the baby is born: the birth makes the mother understand that her daughter was in her womb, in the kingdom of the dead).

Hades like Demeter wants to keep Persephone (*life, energy, sun*), and Zeus concludes that she will be 6 months with Hades (winter of course, but especially death), and 6 months with Demeter (summer of course, but especially life). Here is the human condition summarized in a few lines: human in human time can not be eternal, and must accept frequent passages in the kingdom of the dead cut in half (a piece with the mother and a piece with the father), before reviving.

All that is kept and closed can be opened, and even must be opened by the right person. Cerberus is tricked by a cake of poisoned honey which temporarily puts him to sleep, just as the wolf (of course the mother, who carries in her womb the fetus-girl and the grandmother-placenta) in *the Little Red Riding Hood*, which receives a cake and a small pot of honey (a honey cake, in other words) and goes to bed.

In fact, the placenta (the honey cake, the tree, a yew, whose fruits or arises - the only edible part - have an incomparable taste of honey and of which poison was used for abortions – to trick Cerberus and open his mouth) cause the rational brain of the mother to fall asleep so that birth is feasible and that *the wolves finally opens*. The one who opens, in the tale of *Little Red Riding Hood*, is the hunter. *And precisely.*

The hunter and the placenta are also linked, because the one that triggers the delivery is **the placenta**, it is the one who emits the first *prostaglandins*, a hormone that soften the cervix for childbirth.

First and foremost, the deer and the reindeer are quite equivalent animals. Deer as reindeer have a similar gestation period and an equivalent lovemaking season. They have a very close squad and fights.

The young child receives his antlers, or, I mean his crown at the beginning of the year, like the deer or the reindeer, and now, in autumn, they are ready for battle or to dig up. Like the teeth, antlers grow and grow every year, even if, depending on age (number of lives, glory, importance), they are more or less developed. We enter into the third symbolic pregnancy, which is itself imbricated in the second. Indeed, the second is not yet finished.

Although reindeer was probably more common in Europe during the Ice Age, deer was much more represented in prehistoric caves, which seems to indicate a preference. Probably it was more majestic. The deer stands straight and proud, like a king.

The antlers of deer and reindeer were used as shovel or pick in prehistory (see, for example, *Du galet taillé au bistouri d'obsidienne* by Jean-Luc Piel-Desruisseaux).

It is by knowing this that we must look at what is presented to us.

*Sketches reproducing the painting called **"Le sorcier" (the sorcerer)** or **"le dieu cornu" (the horned god)**, of the cave **Les Trois Frères** (-15,000, France).*

Pan, Cernunnos, Faunus, Hermes, Mercury, Viðarr, deer, goat, horns is, as said before, life, vital energy, and actually adrenaline or more generally hormones.

Adrenaline is a neurotransmitter and a hormone. It is also called epinephrine. Adrenaline is secreted in response to stress or physical activity. Its dispersion in the body causes an acceleration of the heart rhythm, an increase in the speed of contractions of the heart, an increase in blood pressure, dilation of the bronchi and pupils. It responds to an intense need for energy, for example to face some danger: to flee quickly, or fight.

With adrenaline is muscle strength greater, as well as resistance to pain.

Today, scientific names are given to these forces, when they before were given names of gods. You have to realize how much adrenaline is related to life, because it can literally bring back someone who was lost (anaphylactic shock and heart attack). Pan is the vital energy, that is why its name means "Everything", it inhabits everything here on Earth, everything that lives, everything that is transformed, everything that evolves. But Pan, which I also think is adrenalin, the hormone of fighting and fear, is also linked to the term *"panic"*, and You can now understand why...

The panic no longer freezes you, it is stronger than fear, it triggers the deep rise of the adrenaline which causes physical changes allowing you during a short period of time to become a superman, it is in a way, I like to say "the final sprint of life". It responds to a need for intense energy to deal with a danger or a situation of extreme urgency. At a lower dose, it is also secreted when someone is very engaged or interested in a particular subject, so that the brain is fed with an extraordinary energy.

During this time, the heart rate accelerates, the blood is sent first to the noble organs and the muscles (this is why the person generally trembles, which testifies to the exacerbated activity of the muscles). The subject is ready to flee, or to fight.

But there is more.

It plays an essential role in the hormonal balance of natural birth, and thus in *bringing into life*, in what Michel Odent* (French obstetrician and childbirth specialist) calls *the ejection reflex of the fetus*:

*See *L'humanité survivra-t-elle à la médecine ?* in particular.

In the first phase of labor (dilation of the cervix), after the production of prostaglandins by the placenta; the oxytocin produced by the pituitary induces the uterine contractions that cause the opening of the cervix (such as the vulva: it is the wolf's red mouth, which protects the entrance of the grave, the Fenrir wolf in Norse mythology). Pain due to opening of the cervix causes the release of endorphins (natural opiate).

The endorphins reduce pain and project the future mother into a state of trance between the contractions, so that her body can rest. According to Michel Odent, for this balance to be made in the best conditions, it is essential that the parturient (the woman in labor) is in intimacy, in heat and in darkness, which all mammals in delivery are seeking.

Her rational brain must be stimulated as little as possible (no questions, no language, no light), so that her animal brain, her instincts, can take over. In order for a childbirth to take place, under the best possible conditions, social inhibitions must be able to disappear. Thus, the parturient must ideally be alone, she should not feel observed.

Alone, but with a midwife, who, in the dark, is turned on the other side, engaged in a repetitive and simple activity, like knitting, or, I will write more about that later, spinning.

This midwife does not necessarily help the childbirth, in fact she just protects the entrance, she watches. It must be a woman, and a woman who has already lived through childbirth herself. Thus the parturient will be in confidence. The state of childbirth is a real trance, as an intoxication. The woman must then be like an animal. In this state, and at this stage, the adrenaline level will be at its lowest, and that is a good thing, because, at this stage, any release of adrenaline inhibits and slows down the process of delivery, causing maternal and fetal suffering. An adrenaline release can even stop the delivery.

This is quite logical, since if the woman in labor is in a dangerous situation, she must then be able to flee or face, and can not, at the same time, have contractions. Adrenalin is thus the oxytocin antagonist hormone, its release during the labor phase causes in particular haemorrhages of delivery, the leading cause of maternal mortality in the world, all countries combined (WHO, 25%).

In second place, there are infections (WHO, 15%), but at this level they concern only certain countries, with sometimes questionable medical practices; and in third place (second for developed countries) are hypertensive disorders such as eclampsia (WHO, 12%).

Dystocia, or "mechanical" disorder related to childbirth (the baby that does not pass in the pelvis, for example), concerns only 8% (WHO) of maternal deaths in a given population, contrary to what we could believe.

Of course, without Caesarean section, we can imagine that this cause would be more frequent.

Haemorrhage and hypertensive disorders are caused more or less directly by the placenta. This means that in 37% of maternal deaths at least, it is the placenta that kills the mother. The placenta, in our myths: the serpent, the dragon; is a real danger to the mother as well as to the fetus. This is why this final battle must be carried out under the best conditions.

And precisely, in the second part of the labour, at the moment of the expulsion phase, a surge of adrenaline is triggered, which brings a renewal of energy to the future mother, who often adopts a vertical position and seeks grip, sometimes violently. She may feel a sudden thirst, symptom of an adrenaline rush, and she often experiences sudden fear, despair, or an inexplicable urge to run away from childbirth. Often she cries, because of pain and fear, here can we understand the analogy with the wolf, at this time, because it is known for its howling. Note that the wolf, visible in the tale of Little Red Riding Hood, is also seen in many other tales, in a more discreet manner, by its often *screaming howls **that scare children** lost in the forest (the uterus with its placenta) in the tale of Tom Thumb as example.*

This lycanthropic transformation into a wolf and this **panic** announces the complete dilation and the imminent arrival of the baby. The woman then feels a strong urge to push and adrenaline gives her the strength that requires an effective push.

The baby is also affected by this adrenaline secretion **(children *are afraid* of wolves, aren't they?)**: It allows them to adapt to the deprivation of oxygen at the end of childbirth (one of the reasons why this hormonal balance and this final stress is important). Because of adrenaline, he often comes out with wide open eyes and dilated pupils.

Adrenaline at the end of the labour, rather than inhibiting or even stopping the delivery, initiates the expulsion phase and the ejection reflex of the fetus. If she is in a difficult situation, the mother in a too advanced labour, must get the baby out to be able to flee or fight. Michel Odent explains in his books that this knowledge was used, for example, in some Amerindian tribes.

If the midwife, who at a distance *watched without seeing* the labour, felt that the labour was no longer moving forward, then she sent girls to scare the woman, which provoked the ejection reflex of the fetus. This was, and is still used in hospitals, where Michel Odent says that at a time, the midwives and doctors said if the baby didn't want to come out, and that pushes were ineffective: "HEAT UP THE FORCEPS! ". Of course the pregnant woman was *frightened* and expelled the baby without the *above named* forceps.

Not sure she has a good memory of the doctor, or midwives, on the other hand... Adrenaline is very necessary at birth. If it comes naturally, it causes a sensation of fear, and if it does not happen, a fear causes its secretion.

Perhaps you don't understand what these details have to do with mythology, autumn, stag and crown. So let's talk about the god *Pan.*

Pan is especially the god of crowd, of *the hysterical crowd*, because he has the ability to cause his humanity (rational brain) to lose to the panic-stricken person. Pan is at the origin of the word panic, which indicates its anger, but also its taste for the sudden fear that it provokes by its brutal apparitions. If it is known for the terror it inspires, it is also known for the benevolent attention which it carries to the shepherds and their flocks, of which it is the protector. Did I not say this adrenaline stress was essential during birth?

You see here that our modern science is not better than our mythology. Midwives or doctors, screaming "HEAT UP THE FORCEPS!" Merely invoked the god Pan, the terrible but protective god of shepherds and their herds (ancestor-mother and fetus). Only the words have changed.

Among other things, we can say: It is Pan who supplies the dogs (pregnant belly, uterus) to the pack of Artemis (the bear, the mother, *the one who carries*).

Of course, as during childbirth, which is a crazy act, an animal act, the adrenaline secretion plays a central role in the sexual act and the child's conception. Pan-adrenaline is then benevolent and sweeps away inhibitions.

It is said Pan makes mad the one who sees him, just like adrenaline, who can transform you into a ferocious beast, *a werewolf, a berserk.*

Pan is interpreted as a representation of the cycle of the seasons, and **the passage from the sunny season to the autumn and then to the winter.**

In the light of what has been explained, these characteristics are perfectly explained. Pan, Hermes, messenger of the gods, is a hormone, a neurotransmitter, the role is the same, only the words change. While in the god Hermes, the role of messenger is accentuated, and that, thus, incarnates all the hormones; in Pan, the role of adrenaline is preferred.

Childbirth is a ferocious animal moment where pain leaves room only for the primary instincts of the woman, who becomes "wild" and loses its "modern" or "civilized" (dare I say "domesticated"?) appearance. For this reason, Pan, Faunus (*fauna*) is the god related to wild animals. Similarly, the adrenaline rush in general *makes wild*. The panic is explained by adrenaline, the vital force.

He is the protector of the shepherds and their flock, for the shepherd who catches the lambs with his hook is the avatar of the dead ancestor who catches the interest of a child through crystallization in order to reincarnate, so to speak. The shepherd is the one who needs the vital force, and the one who asks for it. The passage from the sunny season to autumn and so winter is explained in the period which is related to this third pregnancy; and finally, we go crazy when we see Pan, because Pan is adrenaline, and adrenaline drives us crazy: which means, aggressive, wild and uninhibited. He is the god of the crowd because the adrenaline rush is highly contagious.

Indeed, Nature has made things such that if you see *a panicked person*, you will panic too, without asking yourself anything, so that if there is a real danger, you don't waste time.

Concerning Artemis, Diana, the bear, and her dogs, as you might expect, we will come back to this, since *this prehistoric symbol is the very object of this book*.

Pan, Hermes, is also the god Loki in Norse mythology. This god is terribly misunderstood. *He* makes the wheel of time turn, it is because of him *something happens* (that is why he is always the one who initiates the adventures): he is the vital force, the impulsivity.

Loki comes from the Indo-European root *luk*, proto-Germanic *Lukan*: *lightning, light, spark*. (See *Sorcery and Religion in Ancient Scandinavia*, by Varg Vikernes.)

Thus, Loki, Pan, the adrenaline, is the vital force, the spark that allows life. He has no *intentions*, he only *provokes*. Loki is also Hephaistos, Vulcan, the one who makes creation possible, with fire (energy). Like a weapon, it contains energy, but *the intention is given by the one who holds it*.

We enter gradually into the third symbolic pregnancy, the last of this year of reincarnation, and the most perilous. In the first symbolic pregnancy, the emphasis was on the beginning of pregnancy, fertilization and development of the embryo. In the second symbolic pregnancy, which is not complete, the focus was on the middle of pregnancy and fetal development, as well as his fight, which begins around the fourth month. In this third symbolic pregnancy, the emphasis is on the exit. The exit of the fetus bathed in this adrenaline and *this force from the gods*, this vital energy, but also the exit of the ancestor from his tomb, for the parallel is obvious.

That is why the fight of the deer, and the symbolism of the horns (the shovel) is so important. At *Le Regourdou* (Neanderthal tomb, -70,000 years old, France), a shovel ... or, I should say, a deer antler is found in a stone wall next to the tomb, *which has been opened.*

"Opened"... Yes, because this shovel is like a modern *key*. The deer in the Celtic tales is the one that leads to the other world, *the reincarnating child* to the ancestor. It is obvious, it is the key, to go to look for the ancestor, *we must follow it.*

The deer, and their footprints (forgive me, I should say *"the strange punctuations"* as archaeologists call them) seem to say "follow me". They are often represented in the caves (*Lascaux* in France for example and *the swimming deer*, or *deer with punctuation*).

It is possible to visit the cave of Lascaux online on the website: www.lascaux.culture.fr.

The deer-headed men, who could be described as horned gods, as well as the god Pan or Cernunnos, already exist (in France, in the cave *Les Trois Frères*, the man is called "the horned god", "the wizard" or "the shaman": this cave also has the representation of a man with buffalo head, *which is the same symbol as the bull*, and other chimeras mix between bison and deer).

Reproduction of a drawing from the Cave of Lascaux.

The punctuation, very common in decorated caves, (visible between the fourth and the fifth deer in the reproduction above), are, I think, an alternate symbol of footprints, much like we would have an arrow today: a sign a lot more enigmatic for those who would not know the bow and arrow, but so obvious to us.

Our ancestors were used to follow the tracks of animals, so for them it was an obvious indication. Especially in the snow, all traces look like a circular hole (classic "punctuation" in rock carvings).

The deer (often a white deer, probably because it is rarer and more majestic, which suggests that it is unique) is the key, it is the one who lets (or not) enter, who leaves or not to enter the third pregnancy.

We find this symbol in his woods, but also more symbolically in deer antler amulets. The deer (the key) and the hunter (the one who tries to open) are very connected. That's why it is a hunter who **opens** the wolf (the grave, the womb) in *Little Red Riding Hood*. The hunter is indeed the one who has the key: antlers (this is still the case today in hunting houses that are often decorated with trophies or stag killings: antlers or deer heads).

Well, that's not all, I did not tell you, but the deer reaches adulthood, for males, *between seven and eight years*... Well, well... And there are precisely seven punctuation between the horns of the deer. This obviously explains why the deer symbol has usually taken over the reindeer symbol (with sexual maturity between two and three years).

It is therefore at seven or eight years that the deer-child has his final crown. The horned god is the weaned child, the adult deer. The key is the weaned child.

But beware, the deer battle (when the deers are adults, when they are *seven years old*) is preceded by *the slab*. The verb *to slab* is *"bramer"* in French, and it comes from the Gothic *Bramjan*, itself very close to the Sanskrit *brāhmaṇa*: *brahman*, that is to say *priest*. The slab is always linked to the hunter. *The hunter is the priest, his function in this ritual is the same: he is the guarantor of passwords, if we remember the man with amnesia at the beginning of the book.*

He will tell if the child knows the right password, and sometimes he will open up the grave. The priest is the one who preserves and protects the material personal effects of the dead, in the living, until he returns. Secrets, passwords, were passed from priest to priest. It's also Pan, the horned god, *the adrenaline, the one who finally opens.* It is also the ancestor himself, who is in the priest and his own password.

The hunter-priest is thus represented by the hunting horn. See on this subject The *Venus with horn* or the *Venus de Laussel (France, -22,000 to -27,000).* That's why Heimdallr blows into the hunting horn to warn the giants in Norse mythology and in the rituals related. The hunting horn symbolically allows you to wake up the dead person and communicate with him, that is to say, as you have understood, let the dead take possession of your body, awaken the dead person in you, and his memories, because the dead is no longer in his grave, but *in you.* Don't forget what we talked about at the beginning of the book: this is not *folklore*, this is as true as what we can often see in modern science. We blow into the hunting horn, we will dig up the dead, to awaken his memories that are dormant *in you*, in the DNA.

The sound of the breath in the horn indicates the hunt, the final fight, the delivery, *Ragnarök, the adrenaline rush.* It's the mother who screams. Very often not a high-pitched cry, but a hoarse and severe "o" sound, characteristic of contractions and then expulsion. This sound is equivalent to *the primordial sound "aum" or "Ymir"*. The same as the one of a hunting horn. The giants, who are also the bones of the pelvis, must then open. It is also the cry of the baby, and *the breath of blood* that it receives by the navel.

It is said of Heimdallr (*Cronos, the time,* but also *Santa Claus*) that he means *pole of the world.* He is the god who keeps the *Bifröst bridge* in Norse mythology: that is to say, the rainbow that separates *Asgard* (the womb) from the lower worlds. It is he who blows in the horn, called *Gjallahorn* if *a danger* (a reference to adrenaline, as always) threatens *Asgard*. During Ragnarök, Heimdallr must kill Loki and be killed by him (Loki kills the pregnancy, and the childbirth destroys adrenaline). He is also the god of the light and the moon, and the son of *the nine virgin mothers*.

One can not be the son of nine mothers, let alone nine *virgin* mothers. Mythology loves riddles, and that's good because I love solving them: it's about pregnancy and its nine months. He has nine mothers because they are nine mothers in nine different time units, and they are "virgins" because they are swelling (see the etymology of *virgin* in the second chapter). Heimdallr is the time (it is said, that he can *see the grass grow* and *hear the wool grow on the sheep*), like Santa Claus, he is the symbol of pregnancy in general.

I will not leave you there. You will still hear me on *Bifröst*. Didn't I tell you that I loved riddles? Etymology will be of no help (*scintillating path*), no, it is its description itself which is useful. Bifröst is a rainbow. In fact, a rainbow is a circle, except that from our point of view, we often see only half of it (from an airplane, you can sometimes see a whole circle, but anyway, a half circle is always, geometrically, part of a circle), and sometimes it is double. A rainbow is ephemeral and fleeting, and it appears, everyone knows, when there is a mixture of water and light. In other words, its symbol is obviously related to childbirth (loss of water and sudden light for the fetus).

The bridge (or tunnel) Bifröst is the open cervix (*cervix uteri* in Latin means *"neck of the uterus"*), which is actually a circle, but that is also called a neck. The fetus can only see the lower part, therefore it is seen as a bridge. Its appearance (its opening) is guarded by Heimdallr (meaning "world tree" and "tree above the bed", the time of pregnancy, when the placenta is over the bed) and it is ephemeral and fleeting (like the cervix that closes quickly after childbirth), it is a scintillating path because it indicates to the baby the way to the light, and it is the most solid work in the world (that's why its opening is so painful).

Note that, as explained above, the horn used as hunting horn serves both to call, to open and to drink (the knowledge, the blood of the placenta, the knowledge of the ancestor). So is Gjallarhorn, Heimdallr's horn.

It is also an avatar of the umbilical cord and placenta (remember that it is the placenta that initiates childbirth especially through the production of progesterone). Indeed, the blood is *both a drink and a breath* (it is the blood that is loaded with oxygen). The sound of the horn is also related to the cry of the newborn baby and who begins to breathe.

How can Heimdallr be the son of nine different mothers? He can because these nine mothers are the nine months of pregnancy, and these nine mothers are *virgins* because they are the avatar of the fetus, as explained before (the fetus being both the unborn and the mother). In addition, these nine mothers are called the ladies of the waves. The sea, the water, is always an avatar of amniotic fluid. In short, Heimdallr, Cronos, is the finished fetus, or the finished character of the fetus, he is the gone time, and he blows into the hunting horn because *he is coming out.*

Heimdallr is also designated by the kenning (in Scandinavian poetry, a paraphrase used as a metaphor) "the white god". The kenning "Heimdallr's head" is also used to designate a sword. Remember, it's Viðarr's sword (Heimdallr's head) that rips Fenrir's mouth (female genitals) during Ragnarök (childbirth). In the same way, a kenning for the head is "Heimdallr's sword". Another nickname of Heimdallr is "the ram". Georges Dumézil suggested on this subject that it is because of this nickname Heimdallr is called "the white god". Another nickname of Heimdallr is "bent stick", which itself is a kenning for "ram". Another nickname is "golden teeth", which is believed to come from the fact that old rams have yellow teeth ...

His head is called the sword or the sword is called the head.

His horn is hidden under the sacred tree (i. e., in the grave).

All humans are called "Heimdallr's children".

Varg Vikernes,
Germansk mytologi og verdensanskuelse

With all due respect to Mr. Dumezil, what he suggests is wrong. The image of the sword tied to the head and the head tied to the sword, as well as the nickname "ram" clearly refers to childbirth (but also to Pan). You should know that childbirth is exactly that: What are called contractions during "the labour" phase are contractions of the uterus that pushes the baby so that he literally hits the cervix with his head to open it.

The white god, which is used again concerning with Baldr (Apollo) is white in my opinion because when it comes out of the womb, the newborn is all white, covered with *vernix caseosa* (in the same way that Snow White is white as snow because she is covered with *vernix caseosa*).

He is called "golden teeth" because from birth he ingests colostrum, and having no teeth, it is this yellow and thick substance that metaphorically takes their place (the teeth have the name of what we eat, that's why the *milk teeth* are called so).

Vernix caseosa is a whitish, greasy waxy substance that covers and protects the skin of newborns. In the uterus, it protects the fetus's skin from amniotic fluid (*the ambrosia* with which the bodies of the gods are anointed, and which is both a food and a liquid) that surrounds it. Premature babies have more vernix than term infants.

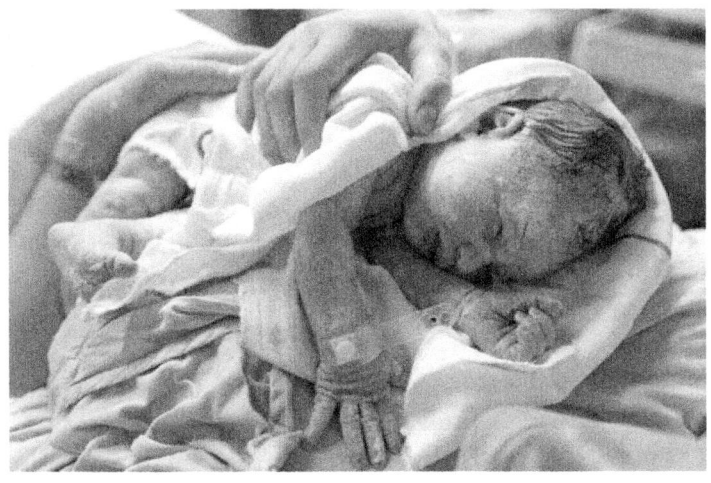

A newborn covered with vernix caseosa. In color, the red - white contrast is often striking. These are the colors of Snow White (which also has dark hair in most versions, like most babies at birth, even if it later blonds) and the goose in the story of Perceval.

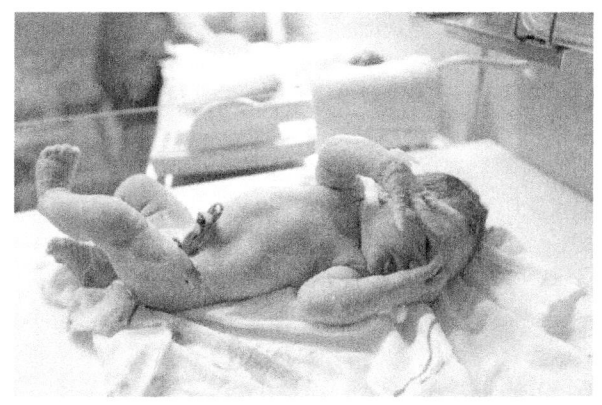

Another newborn partially covered with vernix.

The red clothes of the Kumari are sometimes covered in a white dress, like Santa Claus. She, who very rarely leaves her palace (the house, the uterus), is then carried in a chariot (symbol of the placenta and the uterus: the fetus is still carried).

Heimdallr blows in the horn in time, which, in the image of birth represents the mother and the child screaming; in our faunal symbols: the deer's slab before the fight; and from the point of view of the ancestor: the ritual blow in the hunting horn to announce the exit of the tomb, by digging him with deer antlers. This might well explain why the Bronze lures found in Scandinavia came in a pair: one for the mother screaming, another for the child screaming.

It is said of Heimdallr that he guards *Ásgarðr*, and that he lives in *Himinbjörg*: the castle of the sky, near the *Bifröst bridge* which connects *Ásgarðr* to *Miðgarðr*. Ásgarðr, this fort, this world surrounded by walls, the uterus, is also called, in Norse mythology... *Troy*.

You have understood that, the castle of heaven, Ásgarðr (Troy!), like *Atlantis*, is at once the uterus and the sky, the space. We will come back to that later.

To summarize, autumn retains the image of the final battle of the fetus out of the womb to be born, or here, since it is a symbolic and ritual pregnancy, the battle of the ancestor to get out of his grave (or be pulled out of his grave by himself as a child) and thus relive. This event is closer to the deer or reindeer (and more generally to any horned animal that can hit, such as goat, ibex, ram...), because the antlers were used as a shovel in prehistory, but also closer to the god Pan, Cernunnos, Vidar, who by adrenaline gives life.

The deer is the hunter (but also the placenta, the ancestor and the child himself), the priest, and of course the druid, who cuts the mistletoe, an avatar of the cord (the mistletoe is "bitten" in the tree like a snake), with the sacred golden sickle...

The druid and the priests wear dresses because they are the replacements of... midwives in actual deliveries. They are the ones who make the child give birth to the ancestor's knowledge, those who cure him of amnesia. They are also, with the gods, the only ones who can approach Bifröst and cross it.

If you have heard about the maïeutics of Socrates (also simply called in English "Socratic method"), you are beginning to grasp the complexity of this ritual, and how much ancient philosophy was in fact a philosophy, a science, and a religion. Whether you've heard about it or not, here you will understand something essential...

Maïeutics, in ancient Greek μαιευτική is a technique that consists of interviewing a person to make him express (give birth to) knowledge. It is so called by analogy with the goddess Maïa in Greek mythology, who was responsible for deliveries. The maïeutics is about to make the spirit give birth to their knowledge, to ensure that they themselves find the truths. It is intended to express hidden knowledge in itself. It is thought that this philosophical technique was invented by Socrates, and it is at the heart of his philosophy in dialogue. He thus affirmed that the soul being immortal and always reincarnated, it knew by essence *All*.

The maïeutics relies on a theory of the reminiscence to revive the forgotten knowledge from previous lives.

The term "maïeutics" still refers today to the science of midwives.

"Now my art of midwifery is just like theirs (midwives) in most respects. The difference is that I attend men and not women, and that I watch over the labour of their souls, not of their bodies"

Socrates in *Theatetus*

Socrates explains that the midwife does not give birth to herself, but that she only makes the woman give birth, so does he with the individuals to whom he is talking to.

Maïa, goddess of childbirth and midwives, one of the Pleiades, is mother of Hermes, himself father of Pan.

In Greek mythology, the Pleiades are seven sisters (*i. e.* a seven years old child), daughters of the Titan Atlas and the Oceanide Pleione. They are named as follows:

Maïa, the eldest and mother of Hermes;
Alcyone (or Halcyone);
Asterope (or Stereope);
Céléno (or Célaéno);
Electra;
Taygete;
Merope.

They were the virgin companions of Artemis (the she-Bear, the goddess of hunting and of the moon). During a walk, the warrior Orion (the ancestor) was attracted by their great beauty, and for seven years, chased them (the ancestor must wait seven years before his body is ready: weaned, reasonable, rational). To save them, Zeus turned them into doves (the fetus and the young child are tied to the maternal egg, and symbolized by a bird). It was only at their death that they were placed in the sky to form the Pleiades constellation. At his death, Orion was also represented in heaven, chasing the seven sisters.

The Pleiades are the beneficent fairies in the classic tales (there are seven in the tale of Sleeping Beauty), but also the years of childish and innocent life of course. The beneficent fairies, the godmothers, are the midwives. The evil, old and wrinkled fairy, for its part, is the ancestor, the placenta the one that "catches" the child to "bite" it, but also the unavoidable death of the body.

A midwife (*assisting woman, woman who is with*) can also be called a *maïeutician*. The maïeutics is a profession of taking care of the woman before, during and after childbirth.

The Portrait of a Fairy (1869), by Sophie Gengembre Anderson

Traditionally, this profession is provided by women, often elderly women, who themselves have a personal experience of childbirth. *Michel Odent* explains that she is a figure of the mother (matron), if she is not the mother herself. The care of pregnant women and parturients (woman in labor) is considered almost universally as essentially **belonging to the female circle.**

This role is not exclusively medical or psychological. It is also social and religious. In Christian traditions, it is the midwife who is the godmother, and who presents the child at baptism. She is the one who sees the child first, usually even before the mother, and she sometimes seems to have a magical power of life or death over the unborn child.

Many midwives have been persecuted by the Inquisition.

In the southwestern regions of France, midwifery was reserved f*or the cagotes (excluded population living away from villages, and therefore in forests)*. They had accumulated a much knowledge about medicinal plants, disease prevention and cure, and were then regarded as witches by the Christian authorities.

In 1484, Pope Innocent VIII formulated in the *Malleus Maleficarum* an official declaration against the crime of witchcraft:

"We must not omit to mention the injuries done to children by witch midwives, first by killing them, and secondly by blasphemously offering them to devils. (...) the greatest injuries to the Faith as regards the heresy of witches are done by midwives; and this is made clearer than daylight itself by the confessions of some who were afterwards burned."

They were accused of poisoning, killing and conspiring, but also of healing because their medicine interfered with the will of God. The faithful were only allowed to pray to God and repent, not to heal themselves.

Thus, on this subject, one of the greatest persecutors of witches in England wrote:

"For this must always be remembered, as a conclusion that by Witches we understand not only those which kill and torment, but all Diviners, Charmers, Jugglers, all Wizards, commonly called wise men and wise women (in French midwife is "sage-femme", ie. "wise woman") *and in the same number we record all good Witches, which do no hurt but good, which do not spoil and destroy, but save and deliver. It were a thousand time better for the land if all Witches, but especially the blessing witch, might suffer death."*

Kings and nobility had their own doctors who were often priests, and the church sought to replace the traditional profession with its own clergy. Even today, midwives, these witches, are sometimes poorly regarded, especially by doctors.

According to Larousse (vol 4/6, p 601): « Dans la mythologie romaine, la Maïa grecque se confondit avec une divinité indigène homonyme, déesse de la croissance. Dans la mythologie hindoue, Maïa est la personnalisation féminine du principe créateur. »

In English: "In Roman mythology, the Greek Maïa was confused with a homonym native deity, goddess of growth. In Hindu mythology, Maïa is the feminine personalization of the creative principle."

Her name literally means "little mother", a pseudonym traditionally given to the grandmother, the nanny or the midwife.

We have seen that the deer's slab is the same as the screams of the mother who announce the fight: the birth, it is symbolized by the hunting horn, ritually used to open the doors of the world of the dead (open the uterus during childbirth).

Deer antlers were found on the Neanderthal site of *Regourdou* (France, 70,000 years ago), in the wall next to the tomb, but we can also mention the numerous medallions made of antler found in the Neolithic through all of Europe. The horned gods are not new, we recognize them especially in the Cave *Les Trois-Frères* (France, -15,000 years old), on the *Strettweg charriot* (Austria, 600 BC), in the rock carvings of *Val Camonica* (Alps), on the rocks of *Bohuslän* (Sweden, Bronze Age), we can also mention the tombs decorated with deer antlers in *Hoëdic* (France, -7,500 to -7,000) and *Téviec* (France, - 8,000), and *the cauldron of Gundestrup* (Denmark, about 2nd century BC). This cauldron, which has very clear images, like that of ancestors soaked in water, represents the womb and the placenta. This is the same as the Grail or the cup still given to winners today. Before, the horn was both used to warn, or to blow and to drink; moreover it was a horn: a key, a crown. The winner obtained to drink the blood (wine) of the placenta (the cup) to live again.

Concerning the cauldrons, it is necessary to understand that they always represent the uterus and the placenta, in the tombs.

Thus I explain the human-sized cauldron found in several Celtic tombs (including *the grave of the lady of Vix* in France, dating from the sixth century BC).

Etruscan cup

The cup is also an avatar of the placenta, as the tree, its shape and function are similar.

Midwives help women to give birth. They don't give birth themselves, but make the women give birth. The maïeutics (from Maïa: the growing, enlarged goddess) of Socrates works in the same way, on a spiritual level: the maïeutician gives birth to the spirits, it makes speak their intelligence, or in fact, Socrates indicated it himself, their memory. Weird. Doesn't it remind you of anything? The amnesiac and the doctors I was talking about at the beginning of the book.

In fact, Socrates' philosophy is probably the heir to a tradition that is several tens of thousands of years old, and he doesn't hide it. As in his *Allegory of the Cave*, which is strangely close to the ritual to choose the future Kumaris, he reports and explains ancient traditions and rituals.

But let's go back to the midwives. We are told that during the Inquisition they were considered as witches, and that in fact, they were even the first targets of religious power, who tried to replace them with male doctors, or priests. Witches, really? With a broom? But if they are Maïa, the Pleiade, the seventh, or even the Pleiades, then the witches are also the fairies we know?

Fairies in our traditions, witches for Christians, they are the same. Their broom or stick, is actually a branch of *Cytisus scoparius* or *Scotch Broom*, of the Fabaceaes family. As explained above, they held millenary knowledge related to wild and medicinal plants, that Christianity tried to eliminate. In fact, it is this plant, very common in Europe, which gave its name to the brooms (and not the brooms that gave the name to this plant): in other words, *broom* just means *Cystisus scoparius*. Its branches were used after flowering to make them. A broom, originally, did not even necessarily have a handle, and it was therefore a simple bundle of branches of *Cytisus scoparius*.

The witches didn't use it to fly, although it will be explained why, in the collective imagination, they fly on a broom, but because this plant has other quite extraordinary properties. It is certainly toxic, but like many poisonous plants, in small doses it is used for medicinal purposes. This one can provoke a childbirth. Unlike other abortive plants (such as yew), it is not its poison that, because of digestive spasms and the woman's general malaise, can cause an abortion or childbirth (or kill the woman), but it has *oxytocic properties*, which therefore trigger the contractions of the uterus and *production of oxytocin (the main hormone of childbirth)* in women.

Exactly the same way as modern drugs are intended to trigger childbirth. But that's not all: the consumption (with extreme moderation, the plant is poisonous!) of broom immunizes humans and animals against snake venom (modern confirmatory tests have been performed with viper venom and cobra venom); likewise, it also makes it possible to cure a snake bite, by applying the plant as a poultice on the wound, it will cancel or lessen the effects of the venom.

We use the branch or the flower, yellow, perched at the end of the branch, in a small group, like stars ... Even more striking, these flowers appear in May, the month of Maïa, before giving way to pods filled with seeds (like peas or beans, in the same family).

As a symbol, we could not dream better.

Detail of a branch tip, flower and fruit Cytisus Scoparius or Scotch Broom.

Hermes holding the caduceus (480 BC), Louvre Museum

The caduceus is one of the attributes of the god Hermes (son of Zeus and Maia, and father of Pan) in Greek mythology. It is represented as a laurel or olive stick surmounted by two wings and surrounded by two intertwined serpents. The caduceus is used to heal snake bites and that is why it is adorned with it.

Caduceus, detail.

Without a doubt, the famous caduceus is not originally laurel or olive, but Cytisus scoparius. The Caduceus or Staff of Asclepius, and the Cup of Hygia, which is not so different, has become the emblem of medicine. It is visible on most pharmacies.

Cup of Hygia (Placenta and cordon)

Note the etymology of caduceus, which originally means "to announce" (announcer of birth). From the Latin caduceus, it means *the wand of the herald*: that is to say the one who brings the important messages, the solemn publications, the word is related to the Dorian *κηρύσσω, kērussō* (*"to announce"*).

This wand is the key, like the deer antler, the crown, and the hunter's knife, it allows to open the womb and to bring out the child. It is the one that annihilates the bite of the snake (the umbilical cord), the one that delivers from it.

It is also an avatar of the umbilical cord itself (in a normal delivery it is the umbilical cord that stops beating alone, and therefore delivers from itself), which explains the presence of two or three intertwined serpents (vein and artery) and of course the cup.

The plant was probably often used to avoid too late deliveries, to help the fetus fight Medusa, so to speak: that is to say, help the child out before the placenta calcifies and calcifies the child too. We will talk more about that later.

It is often the midwife who cuts this famous Medusa: this famous umbilical cord, just as the druids cut the mistletoe, the plant (become...) toxic and is a symbol of the umbilical cord. Now you understand why the druids, wizards and sorcerers usually (but even the priests) have dresses. They were maïeuticians, midwives of the mind, in short.

The midwife helps the real woman to give birth, the maïeutician, the sorcerer, the magician, helps the spirit to give birth to the spirit. He is a man but he has a role which in his physical and not symbolic aspect is essentially feminine, so he puts on a robe. The druid, the sorcerer, and perhaps the witch, the midwife, is also the one who kept the passwords, and thus the one who helped open the womb, the grave; the person who gave access. From generation to generation, from initiation to initiation, the passwords left by dead ancestors were secretly transmitted until the ancestor reappeared.

So, his mind, his memory was delivered in the seven years old child.

This tradition of passwords is probably not the oldest, because as the Pleiades suggest, it is the child himself, from year to year and through what I have called crystallization, who gives birth alone to himself, for, at seven years old (Maïa), give birth to the ancestor he was (remember himself). The different Pleiades are simply the names given to the years of the child's life. The appearance, use and preservation of the password allows the ancestor to exist in the child *in the eyes of all.*

All this explains of course why Maïa means *"little mother"*, a nickname given traditionally to the grandmother, the nurse or the midwife. The month of May represents the second symbolic pregnancy, with Easter marking its beginning. This pregnancy is symbolically focused on combat, openness, and this is where we begin to emphasize the importance of the crown, the key. Thus explains the pagan ritual of *the Queen of May*, a tradition preserved in many European countries (especially Scandinavian and Anglo-Saxon and in Spain). As for the cake of kings, a little girl is chosen, as queen for the year, and will be given a crown of flowers.

During celebrations related to the Queen of May, small girls are dancing round.

Little Queen of May, or "Maïa" in Madrid

Strangely close to rituals related to the child goddess Kumari of Nepal ...

Perfect transition to talk to you about another essential symbol related to these famous little midwives: *the bee, the fairy*. Bees are also symbols of fairies, elves, witches and ... midwives.

In fact, if you look at it well, compared to our explanation, the link is already explained: the bees are the midwives of Nature: they open the flowers to help them give birth to their fruit. They are not the ones who create the fruits: they simply help the flower to produce it. The flower is the pregnant plant, the womb of the plant, and is thus the symbol of pregnancy.

All this is even more interesting when you know that this is exactly what the child goddess Kumari gives to all her visitors: she offers flowers and petals of flowers, even crowns of flowers (to the king for example). Bees, these essentially feminine beings are the little Maïeuticians of Nature, every year, and they begin their work seriously in May, precisely. Moreover, these strange beings communicate by dancing and gather at night in the forest, in places known only by them.

They too, to say the least, possess a great knowledge of wild plants, and produce magical drugs (honey). Wild hives of honey bees (in the trunks of the trees-placenta...) are often placed in the intimacy of the forest, in old trees dug by time (including yew, which become hollow and which itself seems to be fed honey, its fruit having kept the taste). The felling of these trees is one of the causes of the disappearance of bees.

But that's not all...

Ängsälvor par Nils Blommér (1850)

This painting shows the elves or fairies (female characters in white dress) in their dance, away from any civilization. This primitive dance seems to be a way for them to communicate. The round shape reminds the bee swarm, which transforms these strange beings into a single communicating entity. The "meetings" of witches or fairies represent particularly swarming, initiated by "the swarm dance" in honey bees.

The broom of the witches, etymologically speaking, is nothing but the *Cytisus scoparius*, as we have previously learned: in French *broom* is *balai*, from ancient French *balain* (*"Scotch broom"*), the Gallic *balatno* (*"broom"*). However, when it got its modern broom form with a handle, it was depicted as a flying tool on which witches sit, and which is almost a part of themselves. It is of course the sting of the bees, *on which they are seated* and which is indispensable *to fly* (for bees, to fly and to live is identical, so it means *to live*: they die when they lose it, because it can break away).

The sting, like the broom, the wand, and the *Cytisus Scoparius* is the key, the object that opens the womb, the grave. In the same way the key is also the crown, the horns, the head of the fetus, which is knocking against the entrance.

Please note that even today, midwives often use a wand to puncture the amniotic bag during labor, to speed up delivery if necessary.

In modern hospitals, hormone swabs, placed in the vagina near the cervix, are also used to trigger childbirth. There is every reason to believe that Cytisus's wand could have been placed in the vagina, possibly with other drugs in the form of ointments (which explains the false witches' penises sometimes referred to in folklore and wrongly attributed to masturbatory acts).
Indeed, in the absence of modern syringue, the mucous membranes are an ideal place to transmit medicinal substances directly into the blood.

It is here the principle of modern suppositories (which in fact, are not modern, since they have existed since ancient Egypt), isn't it?

Sometimes this wand also seems to replace the more classic avatars of the umbilical cord (or even the sexual act, with the "wand" that "opens" the womb to bring in the seed), and its symbolism is mixed with it:

"But being gifted with great powers of foresight, she (the godmother) bethought herself that when the princess came to be awakened, she would be much distressed to find herself all alone in the old castle. And this is what she did.

She touched with her wand everybody (except the king and queen) who was in the castle -- governesses, maids of honor, ladies-in-waiting, gentlemen, officers, stewards, cooks, scullions, errand boys, guards, porters, pages, footmen. She touched likewise all the horses in the stables, with their grooms, the big mastiffs in the courtyard, and little Puff, the pet dog of the princess, who was lying on the bed beside his mistress. The moment she had touched them they all fell asleep, to awaken only at the same moment as their mistress. Thus they would always be ready with their service whenever she should require it."

Sleeping beauty in the wood, by Charles Perrault

This is due to the fact that the wand, like the sting, can be "destructive": like the spear or the arrow, or even the *Cytisus scoparius*, which is a toxic plant, it kills, but this death is absolutely necessary to the getting of a new body, if I may say so, and so it is just a sleep. By the way, the bee kills the flower by fertilizing it. Like Cupid, she throws deadly but beneficial arrows at flowers.

Spirit of the night par John Atkinson Grimshaw (1879)

That's why I have the intuition that these objects, called *bâton percé*, *bâton de commandement*, or *perforated baton* made of antlers or reindeer horns, have something to do with all that. A kind of key, a wand. Note that often are drawn around *the hole* (more often) or *both holes* (less often) what I call for my part... eyes.

There is even one with what I will call... eyelashes, when *archeologists* call them *"incisions"* (*Bâton percé à incisions, Museum of Solutré-Pouilly, France*) - what a lack of poetry! - or a bird's beak, with the hole instead of the eye (*Grottes d'Arudy, - 15,000, Museum of Saint Germain en Laye, France*). There is a nice assortment visible *on the Internet.*

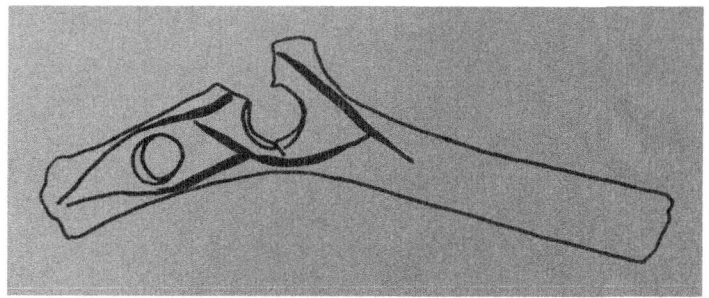

Bâton Percé, Édouard Lartet Collection, France (-19,000 à -12,000)

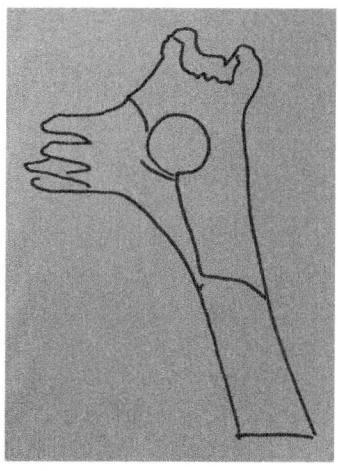

Detail of a carved wooden reindeer stick from the Plantade shelter in Bruniquel, France.

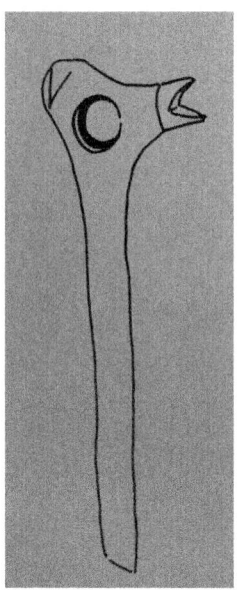

Bâton percé, Arudy cave, France.

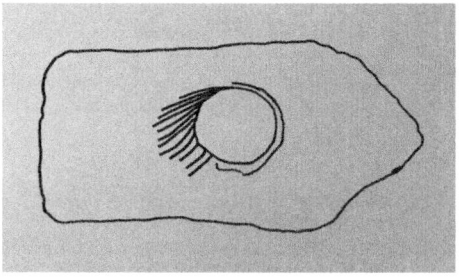

Piece of perforated baton with incisions,
Museum of Prehistory, Grand Site de France Solutré Pouilly
Vergisso, France

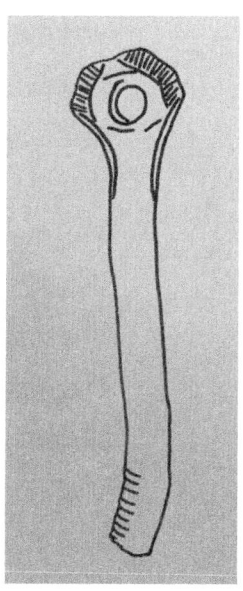

Another perforated baton, Pas-de-l'Echelle, France

As our ancestors explained to us that it was here to put the eye or eyes. Or the sun, the moon? Or both ? Should we understand the name of the goddess Iris (equal to Hermes feminine: hormones, the senses) in that way? the messenger of the gods would simply be... the eye, the iris of the gods? The sun... Because we see with and only with the light. Iris, the bright round, is also the Bifröst bridge and rainbow.

Perhaps these objects had lenses or quartz (crystal or *iris stone*) ball (4,500 year old quartz lenses has been found and were used as eyes on egyptian statues) to concentrate sunlight like a magnifying glass (simple and binocular), like eyes; to be able to, in addition to see the infinitely small in the light of the moon, among other things, burn, like the star of a magic wand?

They are, I believe, closer to this object, equally enigmatic (*ankh: life*, the mirror?):

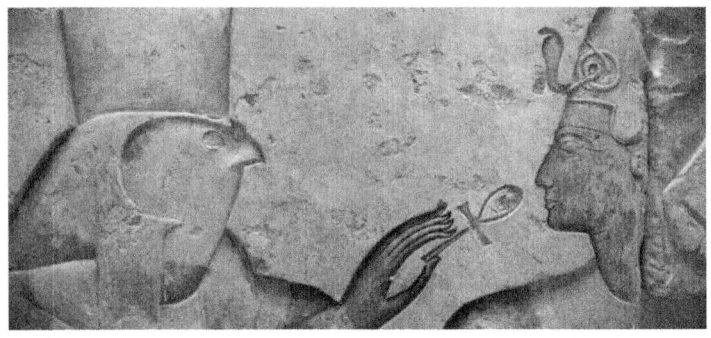

Ankh (Life), mysterious symbol of ancient Egypt

These two objects, with their ring (in French "bague") and their wand (in French "baguette") actually look like... keys (but also masks).

So, fairies and witches are midwives, bees. These characters are much more complex. The witch is of course the image of the dead ancestor and the terrifying Bear too, the famous hooked fingers being the claws, the pointed hat signifying *belonging to the afterlife (understand: to be in the womb, with the amniotic bag on the head)*.

About midwives and witches, and before continuing, I must tell you something. In the myth of Perseus, he questions the moirai to know how to kill the Kraken (*"the one who scratches the bottom of the sea"*). To answer, they have an eye in their hand. An eye in the hand... An eye in the hand? Or a hand that sees? This is of course about a hand that sees. Who can see with her hands if it's not the midwives? And especially when it comes to these themes. In fact we ask the midwife how to kill the placenta (*the one who scrapes the bottom of the sea: the one who scrapes the bottom of the womb*)? She explains that one must cut the umbilical cord (Medusa), or the baby will dry and calcify (will change into stone).

The midwife is the only person who knows how to see in the womb, in the realm of the dead, but not with her eyes, with her fingers, by the touch of the cervix, and also by touching the belly of the pregnant woman. She is therefore the one who sees the future. Of course, the eye in the hand is also the crystal ball, but as the perforated baton (the ring, the cervix, the keyhole by which we can see, in some fairy tales), to which it is linked, it must almost be the subject of another book. The Moirae are Graiae and the Norns in Norse mythology, and oracles, are the midwives, and by extension the witches and wizards.

You will have to follow, I'm not finished. These Nornes, these Moirae, or these Graiae, are represented as spinners or weavers. In my opinion, this is the reason why one of the symbols of the witch is the spider.

Strange, very strange, when we know that *Michel Odent*, a french obstetrician specialist of birth, but certainly not of witches or mythology, explains that during the birth, midwives should knit, or do an similar activity (see among others his book: *Do we need midwives?*). This because, as he explains, the childbirth must happen in privacy, for it to go well, because humans has the distinction of having a highly developed rational and then inhibitor brain, but also because, in its all power, Nature has decided so. The mystery of life must be hidden, otherwise it does not happen. Thus, we say: *the knowledge changes the known object*.

The midwife should ideally be present. Michel Odent says *she must be a protector of the place of birth*. Not only I think he's right, but I'll go further: ***she must block the entrance, keep untouchable the mysteries of life, protect the secrets.***

Michel Odent, for a long time the director of the maternity of Pithiviers in France, explains that he already heard about women who locked themselves in the toilets at the time of the expulsion. Of course, they were dissuaded, but the facts are there: this need for irrational intimacy must be protected, and this is precisely the role of the midwife: *a lock.* Here is her role as a midwife and must be understood to capture the role of druids and wizards in traditional tales. She have to intervene in the process of childbirth only in case of extreme necessity, and she should then only *invoke Pan.*

Invoke Pan! Yes, you understand! This is the reason why midwife-witches are often portrayed as monstrous and inhuman beings. Midwife in French *sage-femme* means *who knows about the woman*. They knew all that, they knew the importance of the adrenaline rush. The children were afraid of them, and the women. And with good reason. The phrase "HEAT UP THE FORCEPS!" Is only *a kind of modern witch*. By saying this, the midwife or doctor puts on her *a witch mask*.

In some European countries, there are customs where a person with a goat mask (Pan) scares children before Yule/Christmas. Goats are also burned on Yule Eve or after Yule. These customs, whose meaning is today forgotten, are reminiscent of Pan's invocation and the adrenaline rush necessary for birth (and thus for the symbolic renaissance of the ancestor in the child).

On the other hand, the appearance of Santa Claus, which is a summary of the phenomenon of childbirth and reincarnation, must remain completely secret. Nobody should see him, or he will potentially not come.

This is the reason why the Nornes, Moirae, or Graiae are likened to spinners (and witches to spiders). Of course they spin the time, they pull the umbilical cord out of the womb, but also, concretely, because they probably spin or weave during deliveries.

They did so because it is a repetitive and benevolent activity. Repetitive activity reduces pain, and as you know, the human brain reacts in much the same way if it sees someone doing something, as if they are doing it themselves. The spinner is also the mother, of course, because she gave the thread to the child.

Through spinning or weaving, mother and midwife become one. By this activity, midwives disappear in the eyes of the mother, while they are physically present. Do you think I poured into psychology? No, this is the actual functioning of the empathic human brain. Moreover, the main quality of a midwife is undoubtedly his empathy. Thus, midwives protect without observing. They are on the watch without looking.

"Here," she continued, "is a chest in which we will put your clothes, your mirror, the things for your toilet, your diamonds and other jewels. I will give you my magic wand. Whenever you have it in your hand, the chest will follow you everywhere, always hidden underground. Whenever you wish to open the chest, as soon as you touch the wand to the ground, the chest will appear.

Donkeyskin (called before: Bearskin), by Charles Perrault

In fact it is not finished, there are other symbols, and not the least. Of course, the opening of the tomb, and the beginning of the last symbolic pregnancy, is Halloween or Samhain among the Celts. Today it is on October 31, or November 1 for Samhain.

During this festival, symbolically the dead return, and children dress up as dead. Yes, that's right, children dress up as ancestors, they disguise themselves as the disappeared themselves. But you will understand everything.

CHAPTER SIX
The Bear and the Ogress: the Metamorphosis

It is only now the bear comes in. You are now entering the oldest depth of the history of our culture. The beginning of the beginnings, if there are any beginnings. The bear is a special animal. To begin with, it is very anthropomorphic. It can walk as a biped, sometimes in a disturbing way, it can sit down and usually nurse his cubs when he is seated, with breasts placed in the same place as those of the women, even if they have four more.

He looks like a disguised human, he often behaves the same way, and eats pretty much the same thing. Historically, for this reason, it is said that where there have been men (in the Northern Hemisphere), there have been bears, and conversely, where there are bears, there may be men. As Nature is redundant, the bear is the natural double of the man, he has the same function. Bears are omnivorous, they are good hunters and feed mostly on plants, fruits and nuts (except for polar bears); like men when they were hunter-gatherers, they have great knowledge of plants, and know what is good for them in Nature.

They are almost herbalists and this learning is a big part of their education, which for this animal is very long (two to three years with the mother). Like the man, the bear is relatively late adult compared to other animals (around *seven years old*, well, precisely...). This very slow development suggests the bear has to go through a lot of learning.

Black bears, after the wintering period, have almost identical measurements to those of humans. The bear has almost no tail, like the human who does not have one. His claws are like fingers and they use them as human hands (with less dexterity). The bear sometimes uses stones and other tools.

The bear's footprints are close to those of humans, even if the foot is more spread out. Like the human, the bear can swim and don't hesitate to go in the water, and above all, he hunts and fishes. They have a relatively big brain compared to their body and they are considered to be one of the smartest animals, even if their post-Christian reputation describes a gruff and silly animal.

The bear, like the Native European man, is adapted to the forest, and above all to the forest, which is its natural biotope.

When they are scared, cubs screams as human babies and the adults are chattering teeth. A bear can easily live thirty years...

Sitting bear

Bear cub standing

There are undoubtedly other analogies. The fact is that the she-bear enters her cave to hibernate in Halloween or Samhain: around October 31st or November 1st. But the most interesting is also that the she-bear is fertilized, often by several males, during the sunny days, from spring to summer (like the cow and bullfights, so there are some male bear fights during the summer). And yet, pregnancy does not start immediately: embryos are created, but she then "freezes" them, so to speak.

It is only when she enters her cave or den to hibernate that she "decides" how many embryos (and *which ones?*) she will develop. She does not have any miscarriage, but *she reabsorbs (devours)* the others. Yes. This depends on how much fat she has stored during the sunny period. At Halloween then, the embryos/cubs, ask, beg their "mother" to be chosen. Choose to be fed until they are born. It does not remind you of anything?

Embryos, of course, are children disguised as ancestors. Should I say ancestors disguised as children? This is the same thing. Still, on this October 31st, they are going in the realm of the dead, in the cave (the tomb, the burial mound), in the womb of the she-Bear, and they are going to implore this terrifying adoptive mother (the Ogress, the witch with hooked nails: the claws) to feed them, as only she can give them life. A treat or a bad spell? (Pregnancy or death?) Yes, today children will beg for candy. Why candies? Because bears are extremely fond of sweet foods, and can eat as much as they want to (in Nature: fruits, honey). Sweets are a kind of transformed sugar (honey), an image of food in the womb of the bear.

You understood. Yes, it is of course the witch in the tale of Hansel and Gretel, with her gingerbread (honey cake) house (the cave, the womb) covered with sweets. The oven is the image of the uterus, which is hot, and which "prepares" the children, who lets them swell, grow, like hot bread or baked cake. The Ogress eats the children because she puts them in her belly. The analogy is there, the symbolism is always the same. So *the big lonely wolf* (*the female reproductive system*, while the she-Bear is almost equivalent to her: the *bear*ing mother) in the story of Little Red Riding Hood she eats the grandmother (the ancestor) and the little girl, before she "spit them out": to revive the grandmother in the little girl, or the little girl impregnated with the grandmother.

Of course, there is an ogress in the tale of *Jack and the Beanstalk*, and of course also an ogress in *Tom Thumb*, and in all the other classic tales. The ogress in the tales has everything of the Bear - and the pregnant woman (the bearing mother)!

She lives in a couple of ogres: the most obvious qualifier to personify a bear, since not only does the ogre eat all the time, but it has to eat all the time, and it is potentially very dangerous. It eats *fresh meat* too. Even more interesting, the bear has extremely good sense of smell but a rather bad sight (or rather, she is very nearsighted), and you will notice in the tales, that it is often easy to hide visually from an ogre, but that this one smells almost systematically "the fresh flesh".

In the same way, the pregnant woman does not see the embryo that *she receives in her house*, she only feels it, smells it, touches it. In addition, the ogre often sleeps, and should not be awake, like the bear.

Well, the ogress is always more conciliatory than her husband. She is even protective. Strange because she is also an ogress... Yes, but if you came in, then you were accepted, you got her favors, you are in her womb and she decided to feed you, in other words, *she chose you*, as an embryo, to grow you in her womb. You will see in the following quotes that the child will systematically ask the ogress for food, like at the Halloween festival, we always face a (often very small: like *Tom Thumb*) hungry child: exactly like an embryo, which only thinks of eating (blood).

Of course she fools her husband, like all the female bear do, because the husband is extremely dangerous, and he is the main risk for the cubs, so she always hides them. This is very well known. The male bear kills and eats all the cubs that are not his. Thus he eliminates the genes of his rivals, and makes the female fertile again, which will enable her to be fertilized with his own genes.

It is thought that this is the reason why the she-Bear is trying to be fertilized by many surrounding males, during the mating season, since she can in any case "choose in secret" which embryo(s) she will grow; but by doing so, the males are fooled and they tend to believe that the cubs of this female they recognize are theirs: thus they don't attack them.

She secretly develops embryos since she does so from the moment she begins to hibernate (hidden in her lair), she gives birth to them secretly, and she protects them their whole childhood, hiding them from male bears (by sending them to climb trees, that the bigger male bears cannot climb).

Yes, that's exactly what happens in the tale of Tom Thumb, when the ogre's seven daughters (actually a single seven-year-old child) are swapped with Tom Thumb and those six brothers (one only child of seven years). The male bear is fooled, he is mistaken and devours his own seven children (his own child).

It must be realized that the Ogress or the witch is present in many places, even if she sometimes *seems* to have been forgotten in some tales, like that of Sleeping Beauty. Often children are hidden at one time or another in an oven (in the womb). The great lone wolf is in a way an avatar of the she-Bear, that is to say, of the mother. The wolf being the female reproductive system, the bear the mother.

Please take note of the following examples, but also pay attention to the fact that the theme of hunting (the hunter is the savior, the one who opens the grave) is almost always present (remember the deer's slab and the hunting horn). Keep in mind the references to the seven-league boots because we will talk about them further:

"What are you doing, my good woman?" asked the princess.
"I am spinning, my pretty child," replied the dame, not knowing who she was.

"Oh, what fun!" rejoined the princess. "How do you do it? Let me try and see if I can do it equally well."

*Partly because she was too hasty, partly because she was a little heedless, but also because the fairy decree had ordained it, no sooner had she seized the spindle than s**he pricked her hand and fell down in a swoon.***

*In great alarm the good dame cried out for help. People came running from every quarter to the princess. They threw water on her face, chafed her with their hands, and rubbed her temples with the royal essence of Hungary. **But nothing would restore her.***

The Princess, the ancestor is dead.

Then the king, who had been brought upstairs by the commotion, remembered the fairy prophecy. Feeling certain that what had happened was inevitable, since the fairies had decreed it, he gave orders that the princess should be placed in the finest apartment in the palace, upon a bed embroidered in gold and silver.

She is buried according to the conveniences.

*You would have thought her an angel, so fair was she to behold. The trance had not taken away the lovely color of her complexion. Her cheeks were delicately flushed, her lips like coral. Her eyes, indeed, were closed, but her gentle breathing could be heard, and it was therefore plain that she was not dead. **The king commanded that she should be left to sleep in peace until the hour of her awakening should come.***

Her memory, her glory is not dead, so she has the opportunity to relive anytime. It is also the symbol of gold: knowledge, memory, gold being the oldest element of our solar system – as far as we know it is created only during the death or the birth of a star. If we think back to the amnesiac of the beginning of the book, she could potentially remember all by touching some gold...

When the accident happened to the princess, the good fairy who had saved her life by condemning her to sleep a hundred years was in the kingdom of Mataquin, twelve thousand leagues away. **She was instantly warned of it, however, by a little dwarf who had a pair of seven-league boots, which are boots that enable one to cover seven leagues at a single step. The fairy set off at once, and within an hour her chariot of fire, drawn by dragons, was seen approaching.**

The chariot, the fire and the dragons are avatars, respectively, of the placenta, the living blood that flows and the umbilical cord. The witch-priestess-mother-helper helps the ancestor to invest a new seven-year-old body. Note the "little" delay of the good fairy.

The king handed her down from her chariot, and she approved of all that he had done. But being gifted with great powers of foresight, she bethought herself that when the princess came to be awakened, she would be much distressed to find herself all alone in the old castle. And this is what she did.

She touched with her wand everybody (except the king and queen) who was in the castle -- governesses, maids of honour, ladies-in-waiting, gentlemen, officers, stewards, cooks, scullions, errand boys, guards, porters, pages, footmen. She touched likewise all the horses in the stables, with their grooms, the big mastiffs in the courtyard, and little Puff, the pet dog of the princess, who was lying on the bed beside his mistress. The moment she had touched them they all fell asleep, to awaken only at the same moment as their mistress. Thus they would always be ready with their service whenever she should require it. The very spits before the fire, loaded with partridges and pheasants, subsided into slumber, and the fire as well. All was done in a moment, for the fairies do not take long over their work.

Then the king and queen kissed their dear child, without waking her, and left the castle. Proclamations were issued, forbidding any approach to it, but these warnings were not needed, for within a quarter of an hour there grew up all round the park so vast a quantity of trees big and small, with interlacing brambles and thorns, that neither man nor beast could penetrate them. The tops alone of the castle towers could be seen, and these only from a distance. Thus did the fairy's magic contrive that the princess, during all the time of her slumber, should have naught whatever to fear from prying eyes.

The dead hero, in the myths, is always accompanied, that's why we often talk about a huge number of people to describe the rebirth of one. In that way is *the Iliad* is the story of reincarnation of a single hero: *Patroclus* (etymology: *"the glory of the father"*) in Achilles* (etymology: *"who has no lips"* because he had never approached the mother's breast, that means, he is the unborn: the fetus), life being personified in *Helen* (*"radiance of the sun"*, that is to say the sight of the sun, the vital energy, as here: *Aurore*, the daughter of the princess is called *Aurore, ie "nascent sun"*).

Moreover, you will see, we are not talking about the reincarnation of the princess, nor about her own death, but about the death of the king, and the reincarnation of the king: it is *he* who lost his daughter, *the brightness of the sun, the sight of the sun, the vital energy*, it is *he* who has lost his life and who must recover it. It's important to understand who plays what role.

*Apollodorus (2nd century BC), III, 13, 6. *"When Thetis had got a babe by Peleus, she wished to make it immortal, and unknown to Peleus she used to hide it in the fire by night in order to destroy the mortal element which the child inherited from its father, but by day she anointed him with ambrosia. But Peleus watched her, and, seeing the child writhing on the fire, he cried out; and Thetis, thus prevented from accomplishing her purpose, forsook her infant son and departed to the Nereids. **Peleus brought the child to Chiron, who received him and fed him on the inwards of lions and wild swine and the marrows of bears, and named him Achilles, because he had not put his lips to the breast;** but before that time his name was Ligyron.*

Of course, the rest of the princess (*life*, the *virgin*, the fetus), death, pregnancy, is directly related to sleep and hibernation. The bear cub being made, developed in the womb during hibernation of the mother, in the cave. By the way, everyone is like *frozen*.

At the end of a hundred years **(100 years is 10, 10 units of time, 10 months of the moon calendar, *ie* 10 months of 28 days, or 280 days, the exact time of a human pregnancy, *i. e.* about 9 solar months with a year cut off in four seasons of three solar months)** *the throne had passed to another family from that of the sleeping princess. One day the king's son chanced to go a-hunting that way, and seeing in the distance some towers* **in the midst of a large and dense forest**, *he asked what they were. His attendants told him in reply the various stories which they had heard. Some said there was an old castle haunted by ghosts, others that all the witches of the neighborhood held their revels there.* **The favorite tale was that in the castle lived an ogre, who carried thither all the children whom he could catch. There he devoured them at his leisure, and since he was the only person who could force a passage through the wood nobody had been able to pursue him.**

Here it is, the ogre. And the hunter. Of course, the forest is the uterus.

While the prince was wondering what to believe, an old peasant took up the tale.

"Your Highness," said he, "more than fifty years ago I heard my father say that in this castle lies a princess, the most beautiful that has ever been seen (Aphrodite, Venus, Freyja). *It is her doom to sleep there for a hundred years, and then to be awakened by a king's son, for whose coming she waits."*

This story excited the young prince. He jumped immediately to the conclusion that it was for him to see so gay an adventure through, and impelled alike by the wish for love and glory, he resolved to set about it on the spot.

Hardly had he taken a step towards the wood when the tall trees, the brambles and the thorns, separated of themselves and made a path for him. He turned in the direction of the castle, and espied it at the end of a long avenue. This avenue he entered, and was surprised to notice that the trees closed up again as soon as he had passed, so that none of his retinue were able to follow him. A young and gallant prince is always brave, however; so he continued on his way, and presently reached a large forecourt.

The sight that now met his gaze was enough to fill him with an icy fear. The silence of the place was dreadful, and death seemed all about him. The recumbent figures of men and animals had all the appearance of being lifeless(...)

It's Halloween, followed by the hunting party (the deer's slab), the boy opens the grave and enters it. Here lies, of course, the bodies without life. Note that the boy decided to go inside after recognizing himself (having taken love for the life he held before): we find again the phenomenon of crystallization, mixed with that of love for the princess-life.

Yes, there is an obvious analogy with the sexual act, preceded by the appearance of Pan-adrenaline (fear).

(...)
until he perceived by the pimply noses and ruddy faces of the porters, that they merely slept. It was plain, too, from their glasses, in which were still some dregs of wine, that they had fallen asleep while drinking.

Of course, since they are fetuses who drink blood: wine is always the avatar of blood given to the fetus in the womb in myths.

The prince made his way into a great courtyard, paved with marble, and mounting the staircase entered the guardroom. Here the guards were lined up on either side in two ranks, their muskets on their shoulders, snoring their hardest. Through several apartments crowded with ladies and gentlemen in waiting, some seated, some standing, but all asleep, he pushed on, and so came at last to a chamber which was decked all over with gold. There he encountered the most beautiful sight he had ever seen.

Reclining upon a bed, the curtains of which on every side were drawn back, was a princess of seemingly some fifteen or sixteen summers, whose radiant beauty had an almost unearthly luster.

Trembling in his admiration he drew near and went on his knees beside her. At the same moment, the hour of disenchantment having come, the princess awoke, and bestowed upon him a look more tender than a first glance might seem to warrant.

"Is it you, dear prince?" she said. "You have been long in coming!"

Charmed by these words, and especially by the manner in which they were said, the prince scarcely knew how to express his delight and gratification. He declared that he loved her better than he loved himself.

We recognize the analogy between the womb and the grave, and the savior, the hunter, the prince, is none other than the boy of seven (the 16 years old princess: 1 + 6 = 7), the young full of life, who comes to wake up himself, and regain his rights, for he has recognized himself.

(…)

They slept but little, however. The princess, indeed, had not much need of sleep, and as soon as morning came the prince took his leave of her. He returned to the city, **and told his father, who was awaiting him with some anxiety, that he had lost himself while hunting in the forest, but had obtained some black bread and cheese from a charcoal burner, in whose hovel he had passed the night.**

His royal father, being of an easygoing nature, believed the tale, but his mother was not so easily hoodwinked. **She noticed that he now went hunting every day, and that he always had an excuse handy when he had slept two or three nights from home. She felt certain, therefore, that he had some love affair.**

Two whole years passed since the marriage of the prince and princess **(up to 18 years: 1 + 8 = 9, 9 months)**, *and during that time they had two children. The first, a daughter, was called "Dawn," while the second, a boy, was named "Day," because he seemed even more beautiful than his sister.*

Dagr ("Day") is also a nickname for Baldr, the most beautiful god of Norse mythology.

Many a time the queen told her son that he ought to settle down in life. She tried in this way to make him confide in her, but he did not dare to trust her with his secret. Despite the affection which he bore her, he was afraid of his mother, for she came of a race of ogres, and the king had only married her for her wealth.

It was whispered at the court that she had ogrish instincts, and that when little children were near her she had the greatest difficulty in the world to keep herself from pouncing on them.

No wonder the prince was reluctant to say a word. But at the end of two years the king died **(just like before... We say: *King is dead, long live the King*)**, *and the prince found himself on the throne. He then made public announcement of his marriage, and went in state to fetch his royal consort from her castle. With her two children beside her she made a triumphal entry into the capital of her husband's realm.*

The first two "symbolic pregnancies" are successful - equal to death and the sexual act, in another symbolic pregnancy - it is the third and the last that will give him all his glory and send him into life, but it is also the most perilous, he must confront his adoptive mother, the Ogress: the Bear.

Some time afterwards the king declared war on his neighbor, the Emperor Cantalabutte. He appointed the queen mother as regent in his absence, and entrusted his wife and children to her care.

He expected to be away at the war for the whole of the summer, and as soon as he was gone the queen mother sent her daughter-in-law and the two children to a country mansion in the forest. This she did that she might be able the more easily to gratify her horrible longings. A few days later she went there and in the evening summoned the chief steward.

Of course, eating only means "having in the womb".

"For my dinner tomorrow," she told him, "I will eat little Dawn."
"Oh, Madam!" exclaimed the steward.
"That is my will," said the queen; and she spoke in the tones of an ogre who longs for raw meat.
"You will serve her with piquant sauce," she added.
The poor man, seeing plainly that it was useless to trifle with an ogress, took his big knife and went up to little Dawn's chamber. She was at that time four years old, and when she came running with a smile to greet him, flinging her arms round his neck and coaxing him to give her some sweets, he burst into tears, and let the knife fall from his hand.

Presently he went down to the yard behind the house, and slaughtered a young lamb. For this he made so delicious a sauce that his mistress declared she had never eaten anything so good.

We find the symbolism of the first pregnancy (which ends with Easter) where the fetus is likened to a lamb. In fact, remember, this is a symbolic ritual. We don't really go back into the womb of our mother, so children are not necessarily "eaten" but they are replaced by analogous animals that will be what they symbolically will be in the womb of their new adoptive mother.

At the same time the steward carried little Dawn to his wife, and bade the latter hide her in the quarters which they had below the yard.

Eight days later **(It is the seventh or eighth day after implantation of the embryo in the uterus the future placenta appears)** *the wicked queen summoned her steward again.*

"For my supper," she announced, "I will eat little Day." **(The little day, the brother, the twin, is the placenta)**

The steward made no answer, being determined to trick her as he had done previously. He went in search of little Day, whom he found with a tiny foil in his hand, making brave passes -- though he was but three years old **(4 + 3 = 7, the Ogress symbolically eats the seven years old child, at Halloween)** *-- at a big monkey. He carried him off to his wife, who stowed him away in hiding with little Dawn. To the ogress the steward served up, in place of Day, a young kid so tender that she found it exceedingly delicious.* **(Second pregnancy, which begins with Easter, but also second symbolic constituent of pregnancy: after the lamb-fetus, the kid-placenta).**

So far, so good. But there came an evening when this evil queen again addressed the steward.

"I have a mind," she said, "to eat the queen with the same sauce as you served with her children."

This time the poor steward despaired of being able to practice another deception. The young queen was twenty years old, without counting the hundred years she had been asleep. Her skin, though white and beautiful, had become a little tough, and what animal could he possibly find that would correspond to her?

He made up his mind that if he would save his own life he must kill the queen, and went upstairs to her apartment determined to do the deed once and for all. Goading himself into a rage he drew his knife and entered the young queen's chamber, but a reluctance to give her no moment of grace made him repeat respectfully the command which he had received from the queen mother.

"Do it! do it!" she cried, baring her neck to him; "carry out the order you have been given! Then once more I shall see my children, my poor children that I loved so much!"

Nothing had been said to her when the children were stolen away, and she believed them to be dead.

The poor steward was overcome by compassion. "No, no, Madam," he declared. "You shall not die, but you shall certainly see your children again. That will be in my quarters, where I have hidden them. I shall make the queen eat a young hind in place of you, and thus trick her once more."

Without more ado he led her to his quarters, and leaving her there to embrace and weep over her children, proceeded to cook a hind with such art that the queen mother ate it for her supper with as much appetite as if it had indeed been the young queen.

The queen mother felt well satisfied with her cruel deeds, and planned to tell the king, on his return, that savage wolves had devoured his consort and his children.

We find during this third pregnancy, the symbolism of the doe, so deer, but also the excuse of the wolf, which is the avatar of the Bear and the mother:

it is she who has eaten all these people. The wolf is the female reproductive system, and the Bear the mother herself. In fact the two are guilty.

The Sleeping Beauty in the Wood, Charles Perrault

The Sleeping Beauty in the Wood

The Princess pricks herself and faints or dies by making a thread, symbol of the umbilical cord...

Night now came on, and there arose a terrible high wind, which made them dreadfully afraid. They fancied they heard on every side of them the howling of wolves coming to eat them up. They scarcely dared to speak or turn their heads. After this, it rained very hard, which drenched them to the skin; their feet slipped at every step they took, and they fell into the mire, getting them muddy all over. **They did not know what to do with their hands.**

We find again the wolf, who is always accused or feared in place of the bear, he is also the one who howls (the mother) and scares (the one who calls Pan). The children are wet and unable to use their hands, like the fetuses, and like, especially, the Tyr god in Norse mythology, a one-armed god because he leaves his hand in the mouth of the wolf Fenrir, the mother... In fact, the image of a being with unusable hands is given to the time when the child is not really physically able to use them, so from the fetus status to seven years old, where the dexterity of the hands is then comparable to that of an adult, without any learning.

Little Thumb climbed to the top of a tree, to see if he could discover anything. Turning his head in every direction, he saw at last a glimmering light, like that of a candle, but a long way from the forest.

The tree is the placenta and its cord: like Jack, he goes up, so he attaches himself to it.

He came down, but from the ground, he could no longer see it no more, which concerned him greatly. However, after walking for some time with his brothers in the direction where he had seen the light, he perceived it again as he came out of the woods.

They came at last to the house where this candle was, but not without many fearful moments, for every time they walked down into a hollow they lost sight of it. They knocked at the door, and a good woman opened it. She asked them what they wanted.

Little Thumb told her they were poor children who had been lost in the forest, and begged her, for God's sake, to give them lodging.

The woman, seeing that they were good looking children, began to weep, and said to them, "Alas, poor babies, where are you from? Do you know that this house belongs to a cruel ogre who eats up little children?"

We have the Bear husband who devours the children, and the female Bear who wants to protect them - even if we sometimes have, as in the tale of *Sleeping Beauty*, an ogress who eats the children, rather than an ogress who hide them... in her belly. You have to understand that the picture is exactly the same.

"Ah! dear madam," answered Little Thumb (who, as well as his brothers, was trembling all over), "what shall we do? If you refuse to let us sleep here then the wolves of the forest surely will devour us tonight. We would prefer the gentleman to eat us, but perhaps he would take pity upon us, especially if you would beg him to."

In any case they are eaten, so it's better that they live too...

The ogre's wife, who believed she could hide them from her husband until morning, let them come in, and had them to warm themselves at a very good fire. There was a whole sheep on the spit, roasting for the ogre's supper.

They warm themselves, we find again the famous oven, that is to say the uterus: she hides them in a warm place. Also here, the first eaten will be the sheep, symbol of the first pregnancy and of the fetus.

After they warmed up a little, they heard three or four great raps at the door. This was the ogre, who was come home. Hearing him, she hid them under the bed and opened the door. The ogre immediately asked if supper was ready and the wine drawn, and then sat down at the table. The sheep was still raw and bloody, but he preferred it that way. He sniffed about to the right and left **(So this Ogre sniffs and smells like... a bear!)***, saying, "I smell fresh meat."*
His wife said, "You can smell the calf which I have just now killed and flayed."

We have again the image of the bear who sniffs and whose flair is not mistaken, although he cannot see well, and we have especially the image of the calf, which is used a second time to hide and replace the child: symbol of the second pregnancy, and placenta (such as the bull-spermatozoon).

"I smell fresh meat, I tell you once more," replied the ogre, looking crossly at his wife, "and there is something here which I do not understand."

*As he spoke these words he got up from the table and went directly to the bed. "Ah, hah!" he said. **"I see then how you would cheat me, you cursed woman;** I don't know why I don't eat you as well. It is fortunate for you that you are tough old carrion.* **(He would have eaten little "ogres" or bear cubs...)** *But here is good game, which has luckily arrived just in time to serve to three ogre friends who are coming here to visit in a day or two."*

With that he dragged them out from under the bed, one by one. The poor children fell upon their knees, and begged his pardon; but they were dealing with one of the cruelest ogres in the world. Far from having any pity on them, he had already devoured them with his eyes. He told his wife that they would be delicate eating with good savory sauce. He then took a large knife, and, approaching the poor children, sharpened it on a large whetstone which he held in his left hand.

He had already taken hold of one of them when his wife said to him, "Why do it now? Is it not tomorrow soon enough?"

"Hold your chatter," said the ogre; *"they will be more tender, if I kill them now."*

"But you have so much meat already," replied his wife. *"You have no need for more. Here are a calf, two sheep, and half a hog."*

The head of the pig or wild boar replaces the placenta because, like him, it scrapes the soil (or the uterus) in search of food. The pig/boar itself, with its big belly is the amniotic bag, attached to the head-placenta. Finally, the pig/boar itself is food, it transforms what it scrapes out of the soil and eats into food for the human-fetus. This symbol is found in many tales and must be understood this way each time.

"That is true," said the ogre. *"Feed them so they don't get too thin, and put them to bed."*

The good woman was overjoyed at this, and offered them a good supper, but they were so afraid that they could not eat a bit. As for the ogre, he sat down to drink, being highly pleased that now he had something special to treat his friends. He drank a dozen glasses more than ordinary, which went to his head and made him sleepy.

The ogre had seven little daughters. These young ogresses all had very fine complexions, because they ate fresh meat like their father; but they had little gray eyes, quite round, hooked noses, and very long sharp teeth, well spaced from each other.

It's understandable that they don't look like humans, but much more like... bear cubs.

As yet they were not overly mischievous, but they showed great promise for it, for they had already bitten little children in order to suck their blood.

They had been put to bed early, all seven in a large bed, and each of them wearing a crown of gold on her head.

A crown, the famous object, the shovel, the horns, which you are given when you are seven years old: it is this crown that will enable you to fight and to dig up the ancestor. It must be understood that there is only one seven-year-old bear (or ogre) cub.

The ogre's wife gave the seven little boys a bed just as large and in the same room, then she went to bed to her husband.

Little Thumb, who had observed that the ogre's daughters had crowns of gold upon their heads, and was afraid lest the ogre should change his mind about not killing them, got up about midnight, and, taking his brothers' caps and his own, went very softly and put them on the heads of the seven little ogresses, after having taken off their crowns of gold, which he put on his own head and his brothers', that the ogre might take them for his daughters, and his daughters for the little boys whom he wanted to kill.

All of this happened according to his plan for, the ogre awakened about midnight and, regretting that he had put off until morning that which he might have done tonight, he hastily got out of bed and picked up his large knife.

His knife was his claws: we find the same image of the knives in *the book of the dead* of Ancient Egypt: *"May they never stab me with their knives, may I never fall helpless into their chambers of torture"*, but remember, the three pregnancies have already passed, now it is about to get rid of the ogre-placenta-ancestor.

"Let us see," he said, "how our little rogues are doing! We'll not make that mistake a second time!"

He then went, groping all the way, into his daughters' room. He came to the bed where the little boys lay. They were all fast asleep except Little Thumb, who was terribly afraid when he felt the ogre feeling about his head, as he had done about his brothers'. Feeling the golden crowns, the ogre said, "That would have been a terrible mistake. Truly, I did drink too much last night."

Then he went to the bed where the girls lay. Finding the boys' caps on them, he said, "Ah, hah, my merry lads, here you are.

Interesting. It is the placenta-ancestor-ogre who gets rid of the fetus against his own will, and who kills himself - he slaughters his own children. The little Tom Thumb has taken the crown(s) because he needs it to get out of the womb (or to dig up himself-the ancestor, which is the same), and he removes his cap, that is to say, the amniotic bag. We notice that the ogre-bear sees very badly.

Let us get to work." So saying, and without further ado, he cut all seven of his daughters' throats. Well pleased with what he had done, he went to bed again to his wife.

As soon as Little Thumb heard the ogre snore, he wakened his brothers and told them to put on their clothes immediately and to follow him. They stole softly down into the garden, and climbed over the wall.

The walls or columns are, as in all myths (Atlantis, Troy, Fenrir)... the gates of the uterus, namely the cervix and the pelvis bones.

They kept running nearly the whole night, trembling all the while, and not knowing which way they were going.

The ogre, when he awoke, said to his wife, "Go upstairs and dress those young rascals who came here last night."

The ogress was very much surprised at this goodness of her husband, not dreaming how he intended that she should dress them, thinking that he had ordered her to go and put their clothes on them, she went up, and was horribly astonished when she saw her seven daughters with their throats cut and lying in their own blood.

She fainted away, for this is the first expedient almost all women find in such cases.

The slaughtered girls are the duplicates of the born children: that is to say the placenta, like their father. They are slaughtered because the cord (the head) is cut. The placenta is considered as the double or the twin of the child, the totem, the ancestor, the one who has to die for the child to be alive. Often the birth is pictured as a fight against the placenta that wants to keep the child not to die, but paradoxically, it is the placenta that causes birth and kills itself. Literally, the placenta is slaughtered and it swims in its blood, at birth, and often because of this more or less hemorrhage, the mother faints.

The ogre, fearing his wife would be too long in doing what he had ordered, went up himself to help her. He was no less amazed than his wife at this frightful spectacle.

"What have I done?" he cried. "Those wretches shall soon pay for this!" He threw a pitcher of water on his wife's face, and, having brought her to herself, cried, "Bring me my seven-league boots at once, so that I can catch them."

We will continue the tale later, and we will explain the symbolism of these famous boots, which, in one way or another, almost always come back in the tales.

Tom Thumb, Charles Perrault

Tom-Thumb

We note that children-embryos-placentas fell asleep while eating, as in the uterus.

So Jack climbed, and he climbed, and he climbed, and he climbed, and he climbed, and he climbed, and he climbed till at last he reached the sky. And when he got there he found a long broad road going as straight as a dart. So he walked along, and he walked along, and he walked along till he came to a great big tall house, and on the doorstep there was a great big tall woman.

"Good morning, mum," says Jack, quite polite-like. "Could you be so kind as to give me some breakfast?" For he hadn't had anything to eat, you know, the night before, and was as hungry as a hunter.

Halloween, the weaned child-embryo is starving. In this version, we notice that Jack calls the ogress mum, and that he is hungry like... a hunter.

"It's breakfast you want, is it?" says the great big tall woman. "It's breakfast you'll be if you don't move off from here. My man is an ogre and there's nothing he likes better than boys broiled on toast. You'd better be moving on or he'll be coming."

Well, the ogre's wife was not half so bad after all. So she took Jack into the kitchen, and gave him a hunk of bread and cheese and a jug of milk. But Jack hadn't half finished these when thump! thump! thump! the whole house began to tremble with the noise of someone coming.

"Goodness gracious me! It's my old man," said the ogre's wife. "What on earth shall I do? Come along quick and jump in here." And she bundled Jack into the oven just as the ogre came in.

He was a big one, to be sure. At his belt he had three calves strung up by the heels, and he unhooked them and threw them down on the table and said, "Here, wife, broil me a couple of these for breakfast.

Other versions say that the ogre enters with a sheep and a bag of gold coins: the famous sheep of the first pregnancy, which is supposed to be a diversion, here it is a calf-fetus, son of the bull-placenta. The male ogre is here also one of the many avatars of the placenta-devourer (he often hunts the food but it is the she-bear-ogre who prepares it to him, and he always wants more, even, sometimes, to eat and kill the whole mother), with his bag (the amniotic bag).

Ah! what's this I smell?
> *Fee-fi-fo-fum,*
> *I smell the blood of an Englishman,*
> *Be he alive, or be he dead,*
> *I'll have his bones to grind my bread."*

"Nonsense, dear," said his wife. "You're dreaming. Or perhaps you smell the scraps of that little boy you liked so much for yesterday's dinner. Here, you go and have a wash and tidy up, and by the time you come back your breakfast'll be ready for you."

So off the ogre went, and Jack was just going to jump out of the oven and run away when the woman told him not. "Wait till he's asleep," says she; "he always has a doze after breakfast."

Well, the ogre had his breakfast, and after that he goes to a big chest and takes out a couple of bags of gold, and down he sits and counts till at last his head began to nod and he began to snore till the whole house shook again.

The ogre-bear eats and sleeps, and again, he does not see well but his sense of smell is excellent. The gold is an avatar of blood, memory-knowledge, and immortality; it is the knowledge transmitted by the blood from the placenta to the fetus. Gold is immortal, it remembers everything.

Then Jack crept out on tiptoe from his oven, and as he was passing the ogre, he took one of the bags of gold under his arm, and off he pelters till he came to the beanstalk, and then he threw down the bag of gold, which, of course, fell into his mother's garden, and then he climbed down and climbed down till at last he got home and told his mother and showed her the gold and said, "Well, mother, wasn't I right about the beans? They are really magical, you see."

Well. I will have to tell you something else. The famous hen with golden eggs, or more precisely goose with golden eggs, is an image that must be understood in the light of another myth: the one of *Mímir* and *Hoenir*. In Norse mythology. Mímir is knowledge, memory, it is a head (the head of the dead ancestor). Hoenir is known to have long legs: sign that he is an analogy of the placenta, with the umbilical cord. Interesting detail when we know that his name means "lure (with singing)" or "hen".

Hens or other birds (like swans and geese) with a long neck is a perfect image for the placenta, which definitely has many aspects. Hoenir communicates with Mímir, he himself is not very clever, but Mímir has an unlimited knowledge, and it is Hoenir who transmits it to him. He is the long-necked goose with the golden eggs: once again gold is the knowledge, the memory, transmitted here, to Jack.

Gold is the oldest known material, and potentially oldest of the universe, *the only material that has seen all*. If we think about the amnesia again, then potentially touching or seeing gold, *we can remember everything*.

(...)

So one fine morning he rose up early **(second symbolic pregnancy)**, *and got onto the beanstalk, and he climbed, and he climbed, and he climbed, and he climbed, and he climbed, and he climbed till at last he came out onto the road again and up to the great tall house he had been to before. There, sure enough, was the great tall woman a-standing on the doorstep.*

"Good morning, mum," says Jack, as bold as brass, "could you be so good as to give me something to eat?"

"Go away, my boy," said the big tall woman, "or else my man will eat you up for breakfast. But aren't you the youngster who came here once before? Do you know, that very day my man missed one of his bags of gold."

"That's strange, mum," said Jack, "I dare say I could tell you something about that, but I'm so hungry I can't speak till I've had something to eat."

Well, the big tall woman was so curious that she took him in and gave him something to eat. But he had scarcely begun munching it as slowly as he could when thump! thump! they heard the giant's footstep, and his wife hid Jack away in the oven. **(The womb)**

All happened as it did before. In came the ogre as he did before, said, "Fee-fi-fo-fum," and had his breakfast off three broiled oxen.

As I told you, second pregnancy, second symbol: the ox, also avatar of the placenta-spermatozoon.

Then he said, "Wife, bring me the hen that lays the golden eggs." So she brought it, and the ogre said, "Lay," and it laid an egg all of gold. And then the ogre began to nod his head, and to snore till the house shook.

Then Jack crept out of the oven on tiptoe and caught hold of the golden hen, and was off before you could say "Jack Robinson." But this time the hen gave a cackle which woke the ogre, and just as Jack got out of the house he heard him calling, "Wife, wife, what have you done with my golden hen?"

And the wife said, "Why, my dear?"

But that was all Jack heard, for he rushed off to the beanstalk and climbed down like a house on fire. And when he got home he showed his mother the wonderful hen, and said "Lay" to it; and it laid a golden egg every time he said "Lay."

(…)

So one fine morning he rose up early and got to the beanstalk **(third symbolic pregnancy)**, *and he climbed, and he climbed, and he climbed, and he climbed till he got to the top.*

But this time he knew better than to go straight to the ogre's house. And when he got near it, he waited behind a bush till he saw the ogre's wife come out with a pail to get some water, and then he crept into the house and got into the copper. He hadn't been there long when he heard thump! thump! thump! as before, and in came the ogre and his wife.

"Fee-fi-fo-fum, I smell the blood of an Englishman," cried out the ogre. "I smell him, wife, I smell him."

"Do you, my dearie?" says the ogre's wife. "Then, if it's that little rogue that stole your gold and the hen that laid the golden eggs he's sure to have got into the oven." And they both rushed to the oven.

But Jack wasn't there, luckily, and the ogre' s wife said, "There you are again with your fee-fi-fo-fum. Why, of course, it's the boy you caught last night that I've just broiled for your breakfast. How forgetful I am, and how careless you are not to know the difference between live and dead after all these years."

So the ogre sat down to the breakfast and ate it, but every now and then he would mutter, "Well, I could have sworn --" and he'd get up and search the larder and the cupboards and everything, only, luckily, he didn't think of the copper.

After breakfast was over, the ogre called out, "Wife, wife, bring me my golden harp."

So she brought it and put it on the table before him. Then he said, "Sing!" and the golden harp sang most beautifully. And it went on singing till the ogre fell asleep, and commenced to snore like thunder.

Then Jack lifted up the copper lid very quietly and got down like a mouse and crept on hands and knees till he came to the table, when up he crawled, caught hold of the golden harp and dashed with it towards the door.

But the harp called out quite loud, "Master! Master!" and the ogre woke up just in time to see Jack running off with his harp.

Jack ran as fast as he could, and the ogre came rushing after, and would soon have caught him, only Jack had a start and dodged him a bit and knew where he was going. When he got to the beanstalk the ogre was not more than twenty yards away when suddenly he saw Jack disappear like, and when he came to the end of the road he saw Jack underneath climbing down for dear life. Well, the ogre didn't like trusting himself to such a ladder, and he stood and waited, so Jack got another start.

But just then the harp cried out, "Master! Master!" and the ogre swung himself down onto the beanstalk, which shook with his weight. Down climbs Jack, and after him climbed the ogre.

By this time Jack had climbed down and climbed down and climbed down till he was very nearly home. So he called out, "Mother! Mother! bring me an ax, bring me an ax." And his mother came rushing out with the ax in her hand, but when she came to the beanstalk she stood stock still with fright, for there she saw the ogre with his legs just through the clouds.

But Jack jumped down and got hold of the ax and gave a chop at the beanstalk which cut it half in two. The ogre felt the beanstalk shake and quiver, so he stopped to see what was the matter. Then Jack gave another chop with the ax, and the beanstalk was cut in two and began to topple over. Then the ogre fell down and broke his crown, and the beanstalk came toppling after.

Then Jack showed his mother his golden harp, and what with showing that and selling the golden eggs, Jack and his mother became very rich, and he married a great princess, and they lived happy ever after.

At birth, the umbilical cord is cut, here it is the bean-tree, the ancestor is the placenta. It is with the harp: the music, the breath, he escapes and with the ax too: the striking and living heart (Thor's hammer)... It is also the heart that cuts the cord and replaces it.

Everything is in gold, I will say almost the music is in gold, Jack, a seven-year-old, is a reincarnated ancestor, and not only does he remember, but his knowledge is infinite and growing (the goose lays gold eggs regularly). Basically, what do we know? We know that the mother transmits knowledge to the fetus (*"Dans le ventre de sa mère, le foetus associe sons et émotions", The Conversation, le 17 mai 2017* - *"In the belly of her mother, the fetus associates sounds and emotions"*, **"Des études montrent que les porcelets asssocient les voix humaines aux émotions de leur mère dès la gestation",** *"Studies shows piglets associate human voices with the emotions of their mother since the gestation"* **Sciences Ouest, Janvier), perhaps the placenta transmits in the same way the knowledge of the father? The ancestor's head seems to do so.**

Jack and the beanstalk

Jack and the beanstalk

The queen-witch of Snow White is also an ogress, the hunter is also a savior:

Then she summoned a huntsman and said to him, "Take Snow-White out into the woods. I never want to see her again. Kill her, and as proof that she is dead bring her lungs and her liver back to me."

The huntsman obeyed and took Snow-White into the woods. He took out his hunting knife and was about to stab it into her innocent heart when she began to cry, saying, "Oh, dear huntsman, let me live. I will run into the wild woods and never come back."

Because she was so beautiful the huntsman took pity on her, and he said, "Run away, you poor child."

He thought, "The wild animals will soon devour you anyway," but still it was as if a stone had fallen from his heart, for he would not have to kill her.

Just then a young boar came running by. He killed it, cut out its lungs and liver, and took them back to the queen as proof of Snow-White's death. The cook had to boil them with salt, and the wicked woman ate them, supposing that she had eaten Snow-White's lungs and liver.

Here too, Snow White is replaced by a boar, the queen eats her lungs and her liver, which makes her... an ogress. The hunter is also the placenta (remember, he destroys himself and delivers the fetus), and it is the placenta that brings back the "dirty" blood from the fetus to the mother.

In practice, the mother actually "eats" this blood.

Snow White

Snow White

In Snow White as in other tales, the forest is the symbol of the uterus, the tree of the placenta. The animals are the companions of the fetus, real or imagined, the bear cubs... These are almost always present, sometimes as humans as in the tale of Sleeping Beauty and sometimes in very large numbers (in the Iliad, for example, the Greeks are actually the companions of Achilles, a fetus to be born or an ancestor to reincarnate).

The Sleeping Snow White, Hans Makart

The resting princess-fetus, white, beautiful and young, and the moving ancestor-placenta, red, old and scary.

"We will set to work on that," said Hansel, "and have a good meal. I will eat a bit of the roof, and you Gretel, can eat some of the window, it will taste sweet." Hansel reached up above, and broke off a little of the roof to try how it tasted, and Gretel leant against the window and nibbled at the panes.
Then a soft voice cried from the parlor -

"Nibble, nibble, gnaw
Who is nibbling at my little house."
The children answered -
"The wind, the wind,
The heaven-born wind,"
and went on eating without disturbing themselves.
Hansel, who liked the taste of the roof, tore down a
great piece of it, and Gretel pushed out the whole of
one round window-pane, sat down, and enjoyed
herself with it. Suddenly the door opened, and a
woman as old as the hills, who supported herself on
crutches, came creeping out. Hansel and Gretel were
so terribly frightened that they let fall what they had
in their hands.

The old woman, however, nodded her head, and said,
"Oh, you dear children, who has brought you here.
Do come in, and stay with me. No harm shall happen
to you." She took them both by the hand, and led them
into her little house. Then good food was set before
them, milk and pancakes, with sugar, apples, and
nuts. Afterwards two pretty little beds were covered
with clean white linen

**Of course, this is Halloween, the hungry children
enter the grave of the ancestor, who is also the
womb of the ogress-bear, and they find food and
sleep there... The suffix "el" added to the names in
German (Hansel and Grethel) suggests that
children are small, like "ette" in French.**

and Hansel and Gretel lay down in them, and thought
they were in heaven.

But they are! For Paradise is precisely the same image of the uterus with its tree-placenta, its snake-cord and its blood-fruit.

The old woman had only pretended to be so kind. She was in reality a wicked witch, who lay in wait for children, and had only built the little house of bread in order to entice them there. When a child fell into her power, she killed it, cooked and ate it, and that was a feast day with her. Witches have red eyes, and cannot see far, but they have a keen scent like the beasts, and are aware when human beings draw near.

When Hansel and Gretel came into her neighborhood, she laughed with malice, and said mockingly, "I have them, they shall not escape me again."

The references to the bear are obvious. She sees very badly, but she smells very well, like a bear.

Early in the morning before the children were awake, she was already up, and when she saw both of them sleeping and looking so pretty, with their plump and rosy cheeks, she muttered to herself, "That will be a dainty mouthful." Then she seized Hansel with her shrivelled hand, carried him into a little stable, and locked him in behind a grated door. Scream as he might, it would not help him.

Indeed, he can not scream in the water, and as a fetus he has no voice.

Hänsel and Grethel

Hänsel and Grethel

Halloween

Transmission: the child-fetus and the placenta-ancestor-bear.

The illustrations are chosen to make you notice how much the tale is similar to the Halloween night tradition.

Let's go back to the symbols of autumn and Halloween, because we have not finished explaining them. For that, I chose as last example the tale of Cinderella. Because there is also a pumpkin. At the next Halloween, you will need to cut and empty a real pumpkin, because the sunlight that shines through and the filaments inside will amaze you, if you've ever seen movies about the life of the fetus inside of her mother's womb. The resemblance is striking.

It is indeed the image of the womb.

The pumpkin or root, with a light inside, is the image of what survives the winter, to revive the plant, either by the root itself or by its seeds. It is a strong image of reincarnation after the *orange* death of autumn. It is the frozen energy, conserved during the winter, the life force. The pumpkin in the Cinderella story is a striking example, it is transformed in a carriage pulled by mouse-servants. The pumpkin is the carriage of the seeds during the winter, and it is eaten and destroyed by the mice, which thus bring to life, or give birth to the seeds.

But in fact ... Roots or pumpkins are substitutes for the real skulls of ancestors.

In the stone age, the children went to fetch the skulls of ancestors, but it was still the case of the Celts also, who were qualified as *"head hunter"* because of the misunderstanding of the Romans in the face of these practices. Missing skulls (and leg bones) are common in graves throughout Europe since the Neanderthal.

When you hear archaeologists talk about a tomb that was probably looted, it probably was *not*, but it was just opened, as it should be in this reincarnation ritual. With Christianity, and sometimes before, this practice ceased, the opening of the tombs became a blasphemy, and the skulls were replaced by roots and pumpkins, symbol of reincarnation.

Cinderella is so named because she lives in the ashes, like Askeladen (Aske = ashes) in the Scandinavian tales, she is a dirty little embers on which one can blow to relive a big and beautiful living fire. Ashes are an excellent insulator, and they keep embers hot a very long time. Thus, ash is the natural avatar of the grave, and the embers, the natural avatar of the dead individual, but still near to relive, thanks to the vital breath: the kiss, the breath, the blood, the music, the cry, the god Pan.

Her godmother, who saw her all in tears, asked her what was the matter.

"I wish I could. I wish I could." She was not able to speak the rest, being interrupted by her tears and sobbing.

This godmother of hers, who was a fairy, said to her, "You wish that you could go to the ball; is it not so?"

"Yes," cried Cinderella, with a great sigh.

"Well," said her godmother, "be but a good girl, and I will contrive that you shall go." Then she took her into her chamber, and said to her, "Run into the garden, and bring me a pumpkin."

If she picks it, we are in autumn.

Cinderella went immediately to gather the finest she could get, and brought it to her godmother, not being able to imagine how this pumpkin could help her go to the ball. Her godmother scooped out all the inside of it **(as for Halloween)***, leaving nothing but the rind. Having done this, she struck the pumpkin with her wand, and it was instantly turned into a fine coach, gilded all over with gold.*

She then went to look into her mousetrap, where she found six mice, all alive, and ordered Cinderella to lift up a little the trapdoor. She gave each mouse, as it went out, a little tap with her wand, and the mouse was that moment turned into a fine horse, which altogether made a very fine set of six horses of a beautiful mouse colored dapple gray.

The fairy, the bee, is responsible for metamorphoses in nature, transforming the elements (flowers into fruits) and at the same time making the most strange preparation possible: honey. Honey is at once sweet, delicious, and refreshing. True honey, derived from flowers, and not from sugar given to bees, has the power to heal, disinfect, and it does not deteriorate itself.

It allows bees to feed themselves, especially during the winter. It is the favorite food of the bear, and in fact, the honey, or the processed honey (candies) is, let's say it now, the ideal symbolic food, after the wine - symbol of the blood - for the fetus and especially the baby.

Since bees (fairies) have the strange power of transforming nature, it is not surprising that they can turn pumpkins into carriages and mice into horses with their wands and stings.

Note that she transforms *underground and scavengers animals* (mouse, rat), so familiar with tombs, in *"living" animals*: horses, par excellence, which are the symbol of the sun, because they are extremely fast, the unicorn being the avatar of light, which "stings through the darkness": its horn is the image of the light that enters the dark... but also and *especially* the horses, the chariots, the unicorn and also Pegasus (the wings are the amniotic bag) are a new avatar of the placenta, arrived by the spermatozoa. The unicorn presents a clear and obvious symbol: its horn looks like a cord with its two arteries and vein twisted. This horn can cure disease and rejuvenate, *just like cord blood that has the unique ability to create stem cells.*

Being at a loss for a coachman, Cinderella said, "I will go and see if there is not a rat in the rat trap that we can turn into a coachman."

"You are right," replied her godmother, "Go and look."

Cinderella brought the trap to her, and in it there were three huge rats. The fairy chose the one which had the largest beard, touched him with her wand, and turned him into a fat, jolly coachman, who had the smartest whiskers that eyes ever beheld.

After that, she said to her, "Go again into the garden, and you will find six lizards behind the watering pot. Bring them to me."

She had no sooner done so but her godmother turned them into six footmen, who skipped up immediately behind the coach, with their liveries all bedaubed with gold and silver, and clung as close behind each other as if they had done nothing else their whole lives. The fairy then said to Cinderella, "Well, you see here an equipage fit to go to the ball with; are you not pleased with it?"

"Oh, yes," she cried; "but must I go in these nasty rags?"

Her godmother then touched her with her wand, and, at the same instant, her clothes turned into cloth of gold and silver, all beset with jewels. This done, she gave her a pair of glass slippers, the prettiest in the whole world. Being thus decked out, she got up into her coach; but her godmother, above all things, commanded her not to stay past midnight, telling her, at the same time, that if she stayed one moment longer, the coach would be a pumpkin again, her horses mice, her coachman a rat, her footmen lizards, and that her clothes would become just as they were before.

Of course, we are only at the first symbolic pregnancy, its appearance is only a dream for the son of the king, because we must not forget that it is in the process to be reborn, and not Cinderella, who is only life, the egg, the virgin, the embers.

She promised her godmother to leave the ball before midnight; and then drove away, scarcely able to contain herself for joy. The king's son, who was told that a great princess, whom nobody knew, had arrived, ran out to receive her. He gave her his hand as she alighted from the coach, and led her into the hall, among all the company. There was immediately a profound silence. Everyone stopped dancing, and the violins ceased to play, so entranced was everyone with the singular beauties of the unknown newcomer. Nothing was then heard but a confused noise of, "How beautiful she is! How beautiful she is!"

The king himself, old as he was, could not help watching her, and telling the queen softly that it was a long time since he had seen so beautiful and lovely a creature.

All the ladies were busied in considering her clothes and headdress, hoping to have some made next day after the same pattern, provided they could find such fine materials and as able hands to make them.

The king's son led her to the most honorable seat, and afterwards took her out to dance with him. She danced so very gracefully that they all more and more admired her. A fine meal was served up, but the young prince ate not a morsel, so intently was he busied in gazing on her.

She went and sat down by her sisters, showing them a thousand civilities, giving them part of the oranges and citrons which the prince had presented her with, which very much surprised them, for they did not know her. While Cinderella was thus amusing her sisters, she heard the clock strike eleven and three-quarters, whereupon she immediately made a courtesy to the company and hurried away as fast as she could.

Arriving home, she ran to seek out her godmother, and, after having thanked her, she said she could not but heartily wish she might go to the ball the next day as well, because the king's son had invited her.

Cinderella

The pumpkin is unequivocally a good example to symbolize the uterus. The light, as I mentioned to you, is the same as that which seems to show in the womb up to the fetus (an orange light, sifted, because we can see the skin by transparency); the filaments inside the pumpkin are like the filaments in the uterus (the endometrium) and feed the fetus. The color is orangey red, and above all, the pumpkin is a carriage. A carriage that allows the seeds (fetuses) to drive through the winter.

Indeed, if you leave a pumpkin outside, it will remain intact until the frosts, which then soften it little by little, to, with moisture, destroy it completely and release the seeds that can, with all this natural fertilizer, sprout in spring, as soon as the sun (vital energy) comes.

In the pumpkins are cut terrifying faces to signify that the ancestor lives in them (the dead skull already has this terrifying aspect), and we put light in it to signify that the vital energy dwells in them (again). It is also to invoke Pan, by fear (we always connect the ancestor with Pan, to revive it. Remember that only Pan has this power). So the ancestor calls Pan, and therefore calls life.

Halloween pumpkins

As for the crown (so the deer or reindeer antler, the shovel to dig up the dead ancestor: the key to open the grave), it is in fact very often present. Either the child is of modest origin and he gets one (as in the tale of Tom Thumb), or he is of royal origin, and he therefore has one *by definition.*

In fact, she is not princess, he is not a prince, she and he are princesses and princes of a year, that is to say, in our present traditions: they have gotten the bean (the beans, the white pebbles) that year, or in other words, they have lost their (first) baby teeth.

The trickery, the inversion of children, refers to this very special peculiarity of the she-bear, which can, in a certain way, choose the embryos she will develop, to give them birth. This notion of choice is very important because it is always present. This is the famous weighing of the soul, in ancient Egypt. This notion of choice is found in the crystallization of the child towards the ancestor. It is not about sins or other Christian concepts, it is about glory, honor, memory and interest raised in the child.

This is the explanation of the gold deposited in the tombs of glorious men: gold keeps the memory, it sees everything and does not lose anything, so if you have a gold jewel on you, it will record your whole life, symbolically, but not only. It is also the symbol of the gold ring, which Donkey Skin deposits on purpose in the cake (the placenta).

This is also why, traditionally, a head is applied on the gold coins, this is the head of the dead, the head of the king: it is *Mómir*, the head, the memory of the dead, *a photograph for eternity*, and what is better than a photograph *to remember*?

CHAPTER SEVEN
The Placenta Twin, the Birth, Dwarfs and Gifts

From October 31st we quickly arrive at Yule/Christmas. *Luckily*, because the actual gestation of the bear only lasts 2 months. So if she goes into hibernation in her cave and starts the development of the chosen embryos to Halloween, then she will give birth to Yule. Yule, which used to be celebrated on the 25th, but on the 25th of the 13-month calendar of our elders, that is to say on the 21st of our calendar: at the winter solstice, during the rebirth of the sun. However, it matters less than one might think, because in the traditions, Yule lasted several days, often thirteen (as thirteen months of the moon/woman calendar: a year).

Yule is the tree. The tree, I told you, is the image of the placenta. But it's more than that. Of course, the Yule tree is the placenta, which is why it is decorated with red balls (bloody food), light (blood avatar), garlands (avatar of the umbilical cord), and often even bear cubs (!).

In fact, the Yule tree is not the tree you know. And yet it is not far: originally it is a yew tree. This unique and eternal tree, endemic to Europe, it has been classified as conifers, and yet it has neither resin nor cones. It has no deciduous leaves, and no real needles either. It has tiny, evergreen, dark green leaves.

It (if we can define it as an individual) can have one or more trunk. Often several, then only one, during its growth.

And then this trunk will become hollow, to form, sometimes, a kind of hut.

It does not have the shape of a conifer, but rather the one of a leafy tree. Still this is not really the case, this tree does not seem to have any real model.

The yew is the ideal symbol for eternity because it is eternal. In any case, we are unable to say how long it can live, and its deadly poison, one of the most dangerous in the plant world, protects it from predators, diseases and degeneration... Fortunately, because this symbol of memory grows extremely slowly. Its deadly poison is everywhere: in the trunk, the roots, the branches, the sap, the needle-leaves, the seeds. It persists even in dry leaves and branches. It is everywhere, except in the aril, the fleshy part of the fruit. An incredibly sweet and sticky fruit, with a unique taste of... honey.

What is incredible is that this poison, *the taxol*, is not just a poison, it's an anti-life. It prevents precisely what is at the origin of life, which makes life possible: it blocks the mechanism of mitosis, *i. e.* the cell division, necessary at the beginning of life, but also all along of it, since the cells are constantly dividing and recreating themselves. We understand then why nothing resists it, not even the cancers against which its poison is used today, but we wonder how it resists himself.

This tree was planted all over Europe, on graves and in cemeteries. It therefore fed on the bodies of the dead, and thus became in a way the dead themselves.

In fact, if you ate the sweet fruits of the tree, you ate a bit of the ancestor, the memory, the knowledge.

We used this tree, since prehistoric times, to make the best bows, this is known, but, in fact, all weapons, if indeed we had enough of it: spears (the one of the fisherman King, in the tale of Perceval: the umbilical cord), the arrows...

All symbols are united in this mysterious tree, poisonous as the snake and nourishing (physical and spiritual or intellectual food). It is the one who transmits life and food, but it also has that awfully dangerous aspect of the one who can take it: through weapons or venom. When we know that trees "manipulate" (and protect) animals and humans, "see", "hear", and communicate through gases and soil fungi (see recent studies on these topics), there is enough to... no longer be astonished by the symbols used by our ancestors, who clearly knew about Nature very well...

Christmas/Yule balls on a fir tree.
They are usually red and gold.

Detail of an yew (taxus baccata) in winter. The black and white on the picture here does not allow us to distinguish the dark green leaves and the fleshy fruit with its bloody red aril.

The balls are avatars of the tree-placenta fruits, often red (Snow White) or gold (the famous golden apples) apples.

In fact, originally, the apples in mythology were sometimes pomegranate, they say. The fruit of the placenta par excellence: they are filled with clots of blood, small red berries.

Christmas/Yule garlands (avatars of the umbilical cord), the tradition wants them of gold (light) or red (blood) color, and often luminous (energy, flowing blood).

The dwarves and bear cubs (fetuses) are frequently used as decorations in the tree-placenta.

However, the symbolism of the placenta is more complex, and the more we draw the threads, the more we find interesting details. So let's explain them. The placenta feeds the child during pregnancy, it takes the food (blood) from the mother, to give it to the fetus. In fact it "eats" the mother on one side, to give on the other side. This is the image of the lioness mentioned before.

Albert Chevalier Tayler, The Christmas Tree (1911)

The placenta grows at the same time as the embryo/fetus, it is present only because the embryo is present, it is a genetic part of the fetus, it leaves shortly after the fetus, and no longer has any reason being. Thus, the placenta is the twin of the baby. The twin who dies to give life. It's strange... Does not it remind you of anything? *Romulus and Remus* of course, but also *Castor* (etymologically speaking, like the animal: *the one who feeds on wood*, tree, placenta: the fetus therefore) and *Pollux, the Gemini.*

But yes, you will understand. Because that's not all. We must look at *Ymir*, the giant of Norse mythology. It is curious, the word *ymir* strangely resembles the word for *twin* in French: *jumeau* (the "j" having a "wet" pronunciation in the Scandinavian countries, and pronouncing it there almost like a French "u": thus *jumeau* would be pronounced "yumeau" and Ymir as in French "umir"). It is all the more curious that Ymir is also called *Ánarr*, that is to say *"the other".* (*Sorcery and Religion in Ancient Scandinavia* by Varg Vikernes et www.norse-mythology.org).

And it's not just an impression, **because the name Ymir comes from Indo-European *ymmó-, proto-Germanic *wumijaz, proto-Nordic *wumjaR, and translates as "twin" as well as "sound", "howling" (of wolves?) and "crying". This theonym is similar to the names of Remus and Romulus and the Indo-Iranian god Yama. Many Indo-European legends tell of the sacrifice or murder of a twin by his brother to create humanity.**

Well...

Ymir is also called *Brimir* (*Brim* means *the hat trick...* Yes, you'll understand), and Brimir in Norse mythology is the hall, the room where there will be plenty of drink. *Abundance of drink*, you read well. It is by the drink (the blood) the placenta nourishes.

He is also called *Aurgelmir*: *the cry, the breath of gold*. In other words, the vital force, the energy of stars transformed into breath.

He is also called *Ölvaldi*, which translates as "manager of the feast" or "manager of the beer"...

Ymir is the primordial being, and the giant founder of the ettins, the giants. He himself was created from the ice of Niflheim (the world of the dead), while it touched the heat of Muspelheim (the world of fire) and melted.

Ettins then came out of Ymir's body, a man and a woman from his armpits, and from his legs a son. Ymir lived thanks to the milk of the cow Auðhumbla. This cow licked the salt and frost of which he was covered, and so appeared Buri, who gave birth to Bor himself. He had three children: Óðinn (*WoðanaR), Víli (*WílijaR) and Vé (*Wíhan), who killed him:

They killed him and threw him into the *Ginnungagap* (*"the gaping chasm"*, the outside). The flood caused by his blood was so great that he killed all the giants, except for the grandson of Ymir (*Bergelmir: "shouting, or blowing in the mountain"*, son of *Þrúðgelmir: "powerful howler"*) and his wife. The mountains being the legs and pelvic bones of the woman giving birth (the powerful howler), as in the meanings of *Perceval* (*who pierces the valley*) and *Vali*; we understand that this is the newborn.

From Ymir's body, Óðinn and his brothers created the Earth. In fact, in traditional practices, the placenta was buried, which means that it was offered to Nature, as food; here the analogy with the world is obvious, like that of the uterus with the space, because it is about the creation of the first man (it is about *your* creation as an individual): so Nature is our twin.

His flesh filled Ginnungagap, his hair became trees, his eyebrow became Miðgarðr, and his bones turned into mountains. In the same way, his teeth and the fragments of his bones became rocks, and his blood gave birth to rivers, lakes, ponds and the sea. His skull formed the sky, which rested on four dwarves, his brain becoming the clouds and the maggots of the flesh engendered the race of the dwarves.

Ymir, it's also a name that looks like the one of Mimir. Do you remember Mimir, the memory, who transmits his knowledge to Hoenir, the hen-swan-goose-placenta, who lays the golden eggs (that is to say, the eggs of knowledge)?

Mímir (*memory, the one who remembers,* from old English *Mimorian,* latin *memor,* from the Indo-European root * *smer-,* * *mer-,* *"remember"*) is known for his wisdom and knowledge. In fact, he is only a head because he is beheaded after the war between the Æsir and the Vanir, but the god Óðinn resurrects his head for advice.

Its head keeps a source under the world-tree, Yggdrasil, which translates as "the terrible horse", the yew tree, the Yule tree, and the very symbol of the placenta, where the placenta is traditionally buried, but also and especially in the grave (we planted a tree on each grave, often an yew). The placenta communicates with the ancestor and transmits memories, knowledge. And did not I tell you that trees can see and remember?

No, names are not alike for nothing, not in Norse mythology. You know, dwarves always have rhyming names when they're in the same family. *Ymir, Brimir, Hymir* ("hymn"), *Mímir* is the same person, and that's very interesting. *Mímir, memory.* We know almost what the mother sends to the child during pregnancy. *Almost.* But there is one question that has not been asked yet: **Who is the placenta?** Yes, genetically speaking, who is it? The mother or the child? I asked myself this one day, we must know, I thought, today, at the time of DNA testing.

And that's what I found: ***The placenta is the father.*** (See the study: *Paternally expressed genes predominate in the placenta* par Xu Wang,a,b,1 Donald C. Miller,c,1 Rebecca Harman,c Douglas F. Antczak,c,2 and Andrew G. Clark, 2013). ***The father's genes build the placenta.*** In a way, the father comes here with his role of transmission, during the pregnancy, he tells things to the fetus.

How did our ancestors know about this? I do not know, but they knew.

The placenta is also the ancestor, the old man, who gives *the last breath of life he can give*, before he dies, slaughtered. Yes, *slaughtered*. Because he will be killed by his twin, the fetus, who fights him at the end of the pregnancy. Do you remember the fighting of the bulls? It's the same thing. The young bull fights with the too old ancestor, to take his place, and in fact, he transmits his breath of life through his death, at the same time.

Yes, since the ancestor-placenta is the same person as the fetus-child, it is also the fetus-child who gives life again, *the breath.* Remember Cinderella, that embers hidden in the ashes on which you must breathe (she must be kissed, like all the princesses to whom we must give life again) to start the fire. It is more the ancestor who blows on the fetus, than the opposite. This is the image of the kiss. The prince kisses the princess, who always represents the fetus, the egg.

The kiss is the mouth-to-mouth, which brings to life the princess often asleep, dead, or fainting. The one who gives the breath is the placenta. It is he who kisses the fetus and who gives him oxygen, and then, in the end it becomes dangerous...

If it is too old (!) *it calcifies*, in other words, it fossilizes... No wonder the placenta is likened to the ancestor who is gradually fossilized in the grave. The placenta is a bit like another head of the fetus, and at birth, you have to kill that head (the umbilical cord, a part, the head, remains attached to the child for a moment. We cut the throat to the snake...).

Remember the seven daughters (actually only one seven years old girl) of the ogre, they were also in a way the twins of the seven boys (actually only one seven years old boy), and they were slaughtered. In the tale of *Hansel and Gretel*, the ogress is put in the oven instead of Hansel. The ogress is her twin, and the old, dangerous and nasty equivalent of Gretel who feeds her brother with her (the benevolent side of the placenta, therefore). The placenta is destroyed, then buried.

In the tale Snow White, it is appropriate to focus on a detail to understand: at the very end of the tale, in one of the versions by the brother Grimm, it is written:

But Snow-white's wicked step-mother was also bidden to the feast, and when she had dressed herself in beautiful clothes she went to her looking-glass and said,
"Looking-glass upon the wall, who is fairest of us all?"

The mirror answered, "O Queen, although you are of beauty rare, The young bride is a thousand times more fair."
The wicked woman uttered a frightful curse, **and she was so afraid, so afraid that she lost her head.**

Snow White

Losing your head has two meanings in French. Here, if one reads the tale simply, one will willingly give it the abstract definition. In other words, *she went crazy.* In fact, it is the actual definition that is involved: the ancestor-sister-twin-placenta lost her head, the umbilical cord has been cut. (We can recognize the appearance of Pan-adrenaline too, because she is *afraid.*)

In her anger she clutched Rapunzel's beautiful hair, seized a pair of scissors -- and snip, snap -- cut it all off. Rapunzel's lovely braids lay on the ground but the witch was not through. She was so angry that she took poor Rapunzel into a desert where she had to live in great grief and misery.

The witch rushed back to the tower and fastened the braids of hair which she had cut off, to the hook of the window, and when the Prince came and cried, "Rapunzel, Rapunzel, let down your hair," she let the hair down. The Prince climbed up to the window, but he did not find his dearest Rapunzel above, but the witch, who gazed at him with a wicked and venomous look.

"Aha!" she cried mockingly, "You've come for Rapunzel but the beautiful bird sits no longer singing in the nest; the cat has got it and will scratch out your eyes as well. Rapunzel is banished and you will never see her again!"

Rapunzel

The cat-placenta witch is indeed Rapunzel's twin, in the tower in her place. Rapunzel, this beautiful singing bird (so who lives, in which the breath is flowing), the fetus, life (I have explained the symbolism of the bird, widely used for this state of life since prehistory) was thrown from the tower (womb) and sent into life: this desert solitude, this miserable and distressing existence. These terms perfectly qualify the condition of the newborn.

Selon le CNRTL (Centre National de Ressources Textuelles et Lexicales), voici la définition de misérable : *Qui inspire la pitié.* ***Et de pitié :*** *Sentiment d'affliction que l'on éprouve pour les maux et les souffrances d'autrui, et qui porte à les (voir) soulager.*

According to the *CNRTL* **(Centre National de Ressources Textuelles et Lexicales :** *National Center of Textual and Lexical Resources*), here is the definition of **miserable**: *Who inspires pity.* And of **pity**: Sentiment of affliction that one feels for the sufferings of others, and makes you want to relieve them.

Here is the definition of **distress**: *state of necessity, need, danger, extreme misery, which can not be prolonged without seriously compromising a health, a balance, an already critical situation. "To cry of distress. "*

But see here: the witch-placenta calls herself a cat. Remember that I had notified one of the placenta avatars as the lioness, the cat.

The dwarf, as I said, is the image of the child-ancestor. Let's say, the ancestor reincarnated, the seven-year-old child carrying the ancestor, his old head. Oh, look, his old head, it is exactly what he kept from the placenta! That is to say the navel (in fact rather the umbilicus, the part of the cord that does not fall before a few days or weeks after birth)? The famous slaughtered head.

Snow White and Rose Red

The classic image of the dwarf (fetus with navel: head of the ancestor) with his beard stuck in a tree trunk (placenta). How can one find better allegory?

This image can be found in the Scandinavian tale *Reve-Enka* (*the fox widow*, transcribed by *Asbjørnsen and Moe*, see the Norwegian animated film *Reveenka*, by *Ivo Caprino*, 1962), where the fox (fetus, red) encounters a old woman (placenta, ancestor), with nose stuck in a tree trunk.

We would not believe it, but very often, even the most innocent traditional tales are telling about the same thing, forming together a great enigma.

It is the head of Mímir, who is sought by Odin, it is the head of the ancestor who is sought by the child, and that, yes, he decapitates, because in prehistory and later in history, the child was really going to look for the skull of the ancestor. And so, he "decapitated" the skeleton.

Thus we find throughout history and since the Neanderthal (*Le Regourdou*, France, - 70,000), buried skeletons, with the head missing. This is when the skull should very often be one of the best preserved element of a skeleton. No, the graves were not looted. Yes, they have been opened.

Very often we can find archaeological traces of these openings, or of some heads recovering, to a state of decomposition which sometimes was not total: hence some of the false accusations of cannibalism in Neanderthal related to traces of knife especially on the skull and sometimes on the legs (*Goyet Cave* in Belgium, and *cave of Krapina* in Croatia -skull-, but also *cave of Isturitz* -skulls- in France, *Chutaltovo* -skull- in Ukraine, *Tautavel* -skull- in France...).

It is the buried himself who came to seek himself, who came to seek his head, his knowledge, his memories. As explained above, it is this head, or the navel, which is *the third eye*, before the child is "blind", "blind" to knowledge, as the prince in the tale of *Rapunzel*, who will only find the sight again when he finds Rapunzel, life. Similarly, the placenta is blind or one-eyed (he only has the famous third eye, the umbilical cord) because he is not alive, he has lost his eyes. The symbol of the dwarf really makes sense with the image of *the child carrying the head of the (often still bearded) ancestor.*

Note that, traditionally, the dwarf is often more or less woodcutter (like the beaver...) and has an ax, symbol of both what cuts the tree-placenta, and the living heart. Axes and similar tools (bifaces, spearhead) were placed on the heart of the dead in the graves of European tradition since the Neanderthal.

Picture taken from the film ForeBears, by Varg Vikernes and myself (available for free on the Internet).
The bodies, since Neanderthal, were often covered with red ocher (avatar of blood), as archeology demonstrates.

Well, I'll give to you the etymology of *Castor* and *Pollux*:

Castor comes from the Greek κάστωρ, *kástôr* whose meaning is *"animal with shiny coat"*, from κέκασμαι the perfect of καίνυμαι (*"to excel, to be brilliant"*). **In the sense of *"animal that feeds on wood"* it is related to κάστον, *káston*: *"wood"*.**

In other words, Castor is the one who feeds on the tree (placenta) and the one who cuts it: the fetus.

Pollux, comes from the Greek *Polydeukès:* Πολυδεύκης: with πολύ, *polý*: *"much, many, very"* and δευκής, *deukês*: *"sweet"*: which means *"very sweet"*.

In other words, the one that is filled with honey and wine, the one that feeds: the placenta (like the witch's or ogress' house).

It is not surprising, in *Little Tom Thumb*'s tale, that he takes off his cap (or his and his six brothers') to put it on the head of the little twin ogress (or the ogress and his six sisters), that simply means he put it on the head of the placenta; and that's exactly what happens at birth. The amniotic bag (the cap, that is why we had the name *Brimir*: *the hat trick*, denoting to the twin Ymir) is indeed attached around the placenta, and opened by the child at birth, it is left to the placenta.

A huntsman was just passing by. He thought it strange that the old woman was snoring so loudly, so he decided come inside, and in the bed there lay the wolf. "This is where I find you, old rascal! said the hunter. It's been a while since I went looking for you..."

He thought the grandmother perhaps still could be saved so he took a pair of scissors and cut open his belly.

He had cut only a few strokes when he saw the red cap shining through. He cut a little more, and the girl jumped out and cried, "Oh, I was so frightened! It was so dark inside the wolf's body!"

And then the grandmother came out alive as well, but she could scarcely breathe.

Little Red Riding Hood

It is indeed a birth: the red fetus, and then, about half an hour later, the placenta, which still beats a little, but not for a long time. The great lone wolf is the avatar of the Bear Mother (her womb and genitals, precisely), who symbolically *bears* the seven-year-old child.

Is it not obvious that this is a birth?

We are therefore in the third pregnancy, begun on the 31ˢᵗ of October, but also in the second, begun at Easter. Both must end at Yule.

In fact not really. The third will end twice, as if to emphasize the "reincarnation" aspect of the ritual and the bear analogy. It will actually be finished at Yule, since the child-ancestor will be reborn, but it will only be *finally finished* in February, four months after its beginning, before the next week of the seven fat days, or possibly in January, when giving the crown to another child.

Why two births? This is what happens to the bear cubs, who are born around Yule, but do not come out of their lairs before February. In fact, one could also say that the second pregnancy ends at Yule, and that the third ends in February, but this is, in my opinion, not right. Yule is really the exit of the womb, the apotheosis, the birth. February is just a confirmation, which ends the year.

We now know that during this third pregnancy, the child entered the grave and decapitated the ancestor. He took his skull, his knowledge, and so he fought the serpent, the dragon, the ogre, the placenta, who, noticing that the child he kept captive no longer holds the end of the thread, the hair, the spear (see Perceval and *the bleeding spear*): the umbilical cord, goes in search of him and drowns, in the amniotic water, and especially in its own blood. Like Ymir and his ettins, drowned in his own blood.

The Girl and the Wolf (1874)

A Variant of the tale of the Little Red Riding Hood, told in July 1874 by Nanette Lévesque.

A little girl was at work in a house to keep two cows. When she had finished her job, she went away. Her master gave her a little cheese and a small loaf of bread.

Oh, did you see that? She was at work in a house to keep two cows, and when she was finished, she went away, that's right, as in the tale of *Jack and the Beanstalk*. She is now weaned, that means, since I tell you, the two cows are the two breasts of the mother, and here is the work finished, she has finished to milk them..., as in the tale of *Jack and the Beanstalk*. She is seven years old, she is weaned, and receives only food from the outside, and adult teeth, teeth from the ancestor that grows in her.

Here, my dear, bring it to your mother. This cheese and that loaf will be for your supper when you arrive at home.

(...)
The wolf started to run, and went to kill the mother and ate her, he ate half, he set the fire on, cooked the other half and closed the door. He went to sleep in the mother's bed.

The girl arrived. She knocked on the door: Ah! my mother, open to me.

- I'm sick my little one. I went to bed. I can not get up and open. Turn the handle. When the little girl turned the handle, opened the door entered the house, the wolf was in his mother's bed.

- Are you sick, mother?

- Yes, I am very sick. And you came from Nostera.

- Yes, I came. They gave me a loaf and a piece of cheese.

- It's fine my little, give me a little piece. The wolf took the piece and ate it, and said to the girl, there is meat on the fire and wine on the table, when you have eaten and drunk, you will come to bed.

The wolf had put the blood of her mother in a bottle, and he had put a glass next to it, half full of blood. He said to her: Eat meat, there is some in the pot; there is wine on the table, you will drink it.

There was a little bird on the window when the little girl ate her mother who said:

- R tin tin tin tin. You eat your mother's meat and you drink her blood. And the little girl says:

- What does he say mum, this bird?

- He says nothing, keeps eating, he has plenty of time to sing.

And when she had eaten and drunk the wolf said to the little girl: Come to bed, little one. Come to bed. You have eaten enough my baby, now and come and lie down with me. I have cold feet you'll warm me.

(...)
- My teeth are to eat you, and he ate her.

Version of Touraine quoted previously, collected in Touraine in France by M. Légot (Revue de l'Avranchin, 1885):

(...)
There she met a very ugly man, leading a sow, and to whom she asked her way, telling her that she was going to see visit her sick grandmother.

(...)
While the little Jeannette was engaged in the chaos of the wrong road, the ugly man, who had just informed her badly, went to the right by the right and short way, then he arrived at the grandmother's house long before her.

He killed the poor woman and put her blood in a bottle ("huche" in french) and went to bed.

His blood, that of the Grandmother, but also his, in French it is "son sang" in both cases: Remember that the placenta is the father, the ancestor.

When the little girl arrived at her grandmother's house, she knocked at the door, opened it, entered, and said: How are you doing, grandma?"

"Not well, my daughter," responded the good-for-nothing who gave the impression that he was suffering and disguised his voice. "Are you hungry?"

"Yes, grandma. What's there to eat?"

"There's some blood in the cupboard. Take the pan and fry it. Then eat it up."

The little girl obeyed.

(...)
While she was frying the blood, she heard some voices that sounded like those of angels from the top of the chimney, and they said: "Ah! Cursed be the little girl who's frying the blood of her grandmother!"

"What are those voices saying, grandmother those voices that are singing from the chimney?"

"Don't listen to them, my daughter, those are just little birds singing in their own language."

(...)
"Ah! my grandmother, why do you have such big teeth?"

"It's better for eating my daughter, it's better for eating."

(...)
Jeannette became scared and said: "Ah! Grandmother, I've got the urge to go (i. e. "take a leak").

"Do it in bed, my daughter. Do it in bed."

"It would be too dirty, grandma! If you're afraid that I might run off, tie a rope around my leg. If you're bothered that I'm outside too long, just pull on the rope, and you can assure yourself that I'm still here."

"You're right my daughter. You're right."

(...)
The monster pulled the rope, but there was no one at the other end.

(...)
"Have you seen that Tomboy girl/that boy-girl with a dog wagging its tail tagging along on this trail?"

in French:
Avez-vous vu passer fillon fillette,
Avec un chien barbette (barbet)
Qui la suivette (suivait)

Like the beaver-fetus, the attribute of the girl-fetus is the dog, itself equivalent to the wolf: as indicated before, the one who guides in the dark, probably one of the first uses of the dog, the best to move in at night without being noticed. The "barbet" dog is a water dog: a marsh hunting dog, he has webbed feet ...

The dog, the wolf is the one who points the way, and who takes the dead to their kingdom. Did not I tell you that the dog, the wolf, avatar of the bear, was a more precise symbol for the vulva and the female reproductive system in general? I think that, like me, you have understood that showing the way to the ancestor is an analogy for the sexual act. The female vulva shows the path to the womb.

(...)
"Yes," said the washers, "we spread a sheet over the water of the river, and she passed over it. - Ah! said the villain, spread a new one so I pass. The washers stretched a sheet over the water and the devil went there with his sow that sank immediately, and he cried "Laps, laps, laps, my big sow, if you do not lap all, we will drown us both. But the sow could not lap everything, and the devil drowned with his sow, and the boy-girl was saved.

The washers are the midwives who welcome the baby, and then the placenta, even if they do not save it and let him bathe in its blood that soaks into the sheet, until it stops to beat.

In the Brothers Grimm version, the following is added:

It is still said that another time, when Little Red Riding Hood was bringing the cake back to his old grandmother, another wolf tried to distract her and get her out of the way. But she kept it well and kept walking straight. When she arrived at her grandmother's house, she told her very quickly that the wolf had come to meet her and that he had wished her good morning, but that he had looked at her with such nasty eyes (remember Pan) :

"If I had not been on the highway, he would have devoured me! you added it."

"Come," said his grandmother, "we're going to close the door and lock it up so he can not come in here. Shortly after, the wolf knocked on the door and shouted:

- Open to me, grandmother! it's me, Little Red Riding Hood, who brings you cakes!

But both kept silent and did not open the door. Gray-Head then walked several times around the house on tiptoe, and, finally, he jumped on the roof, decided to wait until the evening, when Little Red Riding Hood would come out to take advantage of the darkness and eat her.

But the grandmother suspected his intentions. "Take the bucket, my child," she said to Little Red Riding Hood; I cooked sausages yesterday, and you will carry the cooking water in the big stone trough which is in front of the entrance of the house. Little Red Riding Hood carried so many buckets that, finally, the trough was full. Then the good smell of the sausage came to caress the nostrils of the wolf on the roof. He leaned forward so much that he slipped and could no longer hang on. He slid off the roof and fell straight into the stone trough where he drowned. Cheerfully, Little Red Riding Hood went to her house, and no one ever tried to hurt her again.

Well, there are several interesting pictures. In the first place, that of the wolf drowning where little Red Riding Hood had managed to pass. Of course, water represents the water from the amniotic bag that has burst. It is a lot of water. It's the sausage water that Little Red Riding Hood throws into the trough in Grimm's version.

The version from Touraine is interesting, because we see "the washers", which are what we would call today the midwives, they help the Little Red Riding Hood (the fetus) to be born, by spreading a sheet on the amniotic water (thus, the infant "walks on water": anyone who was born has walked on water), while they catch and wrap the placenta that comes after.

The placenta is also the amniotic bag (here the sow: the snout is the placenta, which scratches in the uterus like the sow scratches in the soil, and its body is the amniotic bag), you must understand that it is the same organ, the bag has broken, and the placenta can not close the hole (lap up all the water), then, once out, he lies dead in a pool of water and blood carrying with it torrents of blood; that is why in the imaginary he dies either beheaded or drowned, but he is dead, since shortly after birth, whether the cord is cut or not, it stops beating (because the cord beats, like a heart).

The water pocket is in the uterus, the placenta above, *on the roof, and it goes down through the chimney with its hood (the pocket, the amniotic sac) at birth....*

This is our second image, that of the roof and the chimney.

The house, it must be understood, symbolically is the uterus, and in this one, during a normal pregnancy, the placenta is at the top, not to block the entrance. It is also gradually being sent up as the uterus grows. Of course, it is at the top in relation to us, and under the buttocks or feet of the fetus when the latter is placed upside down.

I say that because it's important. The position in the womb seems to have a kind of unique gravity because of the amniotic fluid, where the fetus can hold the head down while it seems to him ten times heavier when he came out.

In addition, the uterus literally carries the fetus. Like *Atlas* (*"the super-carrier"* etymologically speaking, that's telling...) that carries the globe of the universe. Atlas is gravitation, ours, the one we know, *the one that carries the world, because it must be a force to bring the world.* Everyone, and his enormous weight. Atlas is also the one who reigns over the kingdom of Atlantis, described by Plato in *The Critias*.

Atlantis, as I described in a series of articles on the Internet (www.atala.fr), is a mythical island describing our solar system and its functioning, and the deluge that follows its development is an image of the birth: the loss of water. There is a strong analogy between "heaven", "the universe", and the womb, the exit from "heaven" and birth. It should be known that the Egyptians described the universe as *"the watery abyss of the sky"*. It was understood that there was in the universe a kind of filling element of liquid appearance, or in any case whose gravitational properties were close to those of water. It is undoubtedly this "liquid" that will later give the idea of *"ether"*. We float in the water as we float in the universe.

What/Who carries the world?

In the myth of Atlantis, it is given as a reason for the deluge that the Atlanteans had become too proud. You must understand: it means they were finished, they had no more room. They had filled up the ten kingdoms (10 months of the lunar calendar, 10x28, 280 days, the exact time of pregnancy and 9 solar months), and these were no longer large enough. They must be born after ten months (or nine).

The deluge is found in many cultures and it is always the image of the flood of birth: the rupture of the amniotic bag which brings the infant into a new dimension, a new force of gravity, symbolically.

Atlas carrying the world

The one who *bears* during these symbolic pregnancies, and especially during the third and last pregnancy, is *the Bear*. You already know that the Bear is linked to the sky, because of the most easily recognizable constellation in the sky, and that which, in the northern hemisphere is always present, in winter as in summer: the Great Bear. At the origin (indeterminate), the name "Great Bear" probably did not designate a constellation, but the whole sky. Here is the Great Bear that carries us all: Mother Bear, the gravitational force.

Note that the known stars of the current Great Bear do not look like a Bear at all and are seven in number, it is also because of that there exists the term *"septentriones"* (from latin *septem: seven*) which means "Nordic", indeed, this Great Bear, which is not one, turn around the North Pole. These are the seven lights that show the way to the ancestors (the North being the place of sleep and death).

What interests us even more now, and you will see why I am talking about that, is that in many countries, this Great Bear was called, not *the pan*, like today, but for example the Romans called it *septem triones* that is to say "the seven plowing oxen".

In the United Kingdom, it is called *the Plough*, in Scandinavia, *Karlsvognen: "the vehicle of man"*, in Brittany *Karr kamm: "crooked carriage"*, *Karr Arzhur: "the chariot of the King Arthur"* or *Lost-arar: "the end of the plow"*.

"The vehicle", *"the chariot"* or even, *King Arthur's chariot*, *Arthur* meaning *"bear"*... **And why not the sled?**

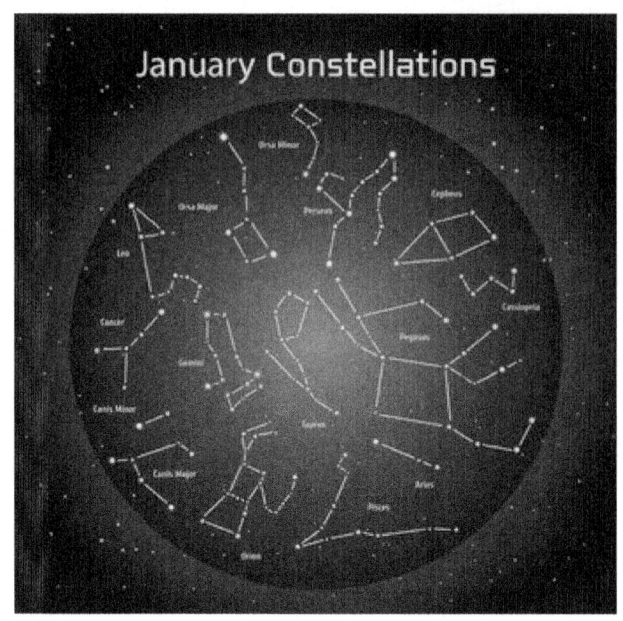

The constellation of the Great Bear (Ursa Major) in a sky map. We distinguish the seven stars and the form of carriage (or pan...).

The constellation Ursa Major, photograph: we distinguish the seven stars.

Chariot (Placenta) of the virgin goddess Kumari (fetus)

Chariot (Placenta, Chernobog) of Apollo (Belobog, Baldr, the newborn "white god") coming out of the waters (amniotic fluid), Palace of Versailles, France

Like the four wheels, the chariot of Apollo has four horses,
Palace of Versailles, France

Many are the ideas expressed to explain the strange form of this constellation compared to its name. There are many who incorporate other stars in the classic seven stars of *Ursa Major*, to find paws, and even a small tail to the animal. Some evoke the long neck of the polar bear. Yet the names given to this constellation in history speak for themselves.

This constellation does not look like a bear, because it represents not the bear, but its chariot, its sledge, which always comes from the North Pole. It is indeed this one, *the Star of the Shepherd* (the ancestor).

Here too, there is a feeling of roof. In the northern hemisphere, this constellation is extremely easy to recognize and represents in a way the lid of the world.

So you understand that this chariot, this sled is the placenta, the ancestor, and that during the deluge it goes down, "by the chimney" to let the infant enter a new dimension, a new world, where the gravitational force is not the same. This is exactly why, in my opinion, birth is unconditionally at Yule, when "Santa Claus" comes with his sled down from the North Pole, then through the chimney from the roof.

The chariot, like the horses, Pegasus, the unicorn, but also the Trojan horse (brought by *the many Greeks, the genes of the father*, in the city of Troy, the labyrinth, the fortified city: the uterus) are always an image of the placenta, the one who carries the ancestor and his knowledge, the one who carries the sitting child-fetus on his back. You can see that the constellation has a shape close to that of the placenta and its cord, and of a chariot with its reindeer.

Statue of Pegasus (etymology: "fountain, spring", another avatar of Placenta), Poland
Should I again clarify that the amniotic fluid is made by the placenta-mniotic bag, which flows, which oozes?

The unicorn, four legs like four wheels. A wonderful symbol of the placenta and its cord.
The horse is the one who bears and heals or gives life. It can also be a goat (Pan, the life force) or a mix of both.

Nuit étoilée sur le Rhone (Starry Night on the Rhone) by Vincent Van Gogh (1853-1890): We vaguely distinguishe the image of the Great Bear, emblem of the night sky.

*Traditional and popular representation of Santa Claus in his
sleigh. In the sky, is the comparison with the Great Bear not
obvious now?*

It is also Þórr's chariot, pulled by his two goats who
have the ability to relive after being eaten, as long as
nobody break the bones of their legs. Exactly like the
dead, whose legs bones, symbolically must be intact,
and returned to the upright position or taken during
the reincarnation ritual of the ancestor, because it is
these bones that carry the man, and that thus are
symbol of life.

In *Le Regourdou*, in France, in the Neanderthal tomb, the bones of the skeleton's legs were thus removed and exchanged with bones of a brown bear's legs.

The Great Bear therefore has the same role as Atlas, this "super-carrier" is the gravitational force, the one who carries the world, the universe, and the one who carries life and carries us. It is not a "mother goddess" properly speaking, as we often hear in prehistoric and historical discussions, as if the beliefs of those ancient times were so simplistic. This is an explanation, as what is called "science" today, it is a real force, which really *bears* us, and allows us to live.

Who better than a bear could embody this role? The bear is one of the strongest animals, his force is formidable, and at the same time he is so human. He is so terrifying, and at the same time so maternal.

In fact, in English, the word "bear" is the same as the verb "to bear"; and this is not a coincidence, the etymology is the same, according to *the Online Etymology Dictionary*:

To bear (verb):
Old English *beran* *"to bear, bring; bring forth, produce; to endure, sustain; to wear"* (class IV strong verb; past tense *bær*, past participle *boren*), from Proto-Germanic **beran* (cognates: Old Saxon *beran*, Old Frisian *bera*, Old High German *beran*, German *gebären*, **Old Norse *bera*, Gothic *bairan* "to carry, bear, give birth to"), <u>from PIE root **bher-*</u> **meaning both *"give birth"* (though only English and German strongly retain this sense, and Russian has *beremennaya* *"pregnant"*) and *"carry a burden, bring"*.**

Ball bearings "bear" the friction. Many senses are from notion of "move onward by pressure."

In a way, not only gravitational force, but added movement.

Bear (noun)
*Old English bera "bear", from Proto-Germanic *beron, literally "the brown (one)" (cognates: Old Norse björn, Middle Dutch bere, Dutch beer, Old High German bero, German Bär),* **from PIE *bher- "bright, brown"**.

The Indo-European origin is thus identical: it is the root (PIE root) * bher- which means *"bear, to bear, pregnant, give birth to, carry a burden; but also brilliant (like the stars ...), brown "*.

Still something interesting, as I explained previously, the bear, an unpredictable and dangerous animal, was and probably has always been more or less feared and revered. This explains why his name has always been taboo. In Yves Salingue's book *La Quête de l'Ours* (*Quest for the Bear*), the author explains that the bear is traditionally never named, because we might then call it. Similarly, in tales and stories, he was systematically replaced by an allegory (the ogre, the big wolf, the Fisherman King...).

This also reveals why our tales and traditions only very rarely directly retain the image of the bear, whereas this one is in fact the center of the beginnings of European culture, for tens of thousands of years, before (and even during ...) the appearance of Christianity. The *Online Etymology Dictionary* describes exactly the same phenomenon:

Greek arktos and Latin ursus retain **the PIE root word for "bear" (*rtko; see Arctic)**, but **it is believed to have been ritually replaced in the northern branches because of hunters' taboo on names of wild animals** (compare the Irish equivalent *"the good calf"*, Welsh *"honey-pig,"* Lithuanian *"the licker,"* Russian *medved "honey-eater"*). Others connect the Germanic word with Latin ferus "wild," as if it meant "the wild animal (par excellence) of the northern woods."

In French and English, you now know that in fact, even though we use the word "bear", directly from the famous taboo root, he is also "the ogre", "the big wolf", "the lone wolf" , "the Fisherman King", etc.

As the dictionary tells us that the word *Arktos* (*bear* in Greek) is in fact drawn from the same root, and suggests we go read the information related to the word *"Arctic"*, I read it:

Arctic (adj.):
Artik, from Old French *artique*, from Medieval Latin *articus*, from Latin *arcticus*, from Greek *arktikos* **"of the north,"** literally **"of the (constellation) Bear,"** from arktos **"bear; Ursa Major; the region of the north,"** the Bear being a northerly constellation. From *rkto-, the usual Indo-European base for **"bear"** (source also of Avestan aresho, Armenian arj, Albanian ari, Latin ursus, Welsh arth); see bear (n.) for why the name changed in Germanic. The -c- was restored from 1550s. As a noun, "the Arctic regions," from 1560s.

This constellation is the oldest. The origin of its name is officially unknown.

Understand, then, that "the sky", the universe, is an image of the uterus in which we find ourselves, and where we have received life. Its equivalent is the uterus that gives life to the fetus. Its symbol is the bear, who is so strong that he seems to be able to carry the world. Of course, this is why the so-called Paradise is symbolically in the sky, and actually in the womb, where we are naked but with no defined gender, and we eat in abundance the fruits of the tree (placenta) offered by the snake (the umbilical cord).

As usual, Christianity reveals the pagan symbols, stolen but often denigrated, demonized. This fruit of knowledge (remember *Mimir,* the head of the ancestor, the placenta, which transmits knowledge, and eggs of gold) is therefore seen as a sin, while it was obviously not the case in our traditions, it was on the contrary the essence of the European man, his culture and his science.

In no case, for a fetus, to eat the fruit of the placenta could be a transgression of the divine law. *It was precisely the divine law itself.*

Regarding the philosophical problem of original sin, I recommend you my first book *Le besoin d'impossible*, written in 2009.

The constellation Ursa Major is therefore the horse, the chariot, the sleigh of the ancestor, of the (She-) Bear: that is to say the placenta.

So he comes down from the sky at Yule, Santa Claus. He who at the same time represents the mother, the ancestor, the benevolent gravitation, the nourishing placenta, the knowledge, and even the body of the child, the new himself. He who is at the same time benevolent and terrifying, because the infinite is terrifying and vertiginous (remember the number Pi) and because of the god Pan (the famous *Father Whipper*), the spark, the adrenaline, which is indispensable to life. It is a synthesis of everything that has been described so far, and it has all the symbols.

Even going down the chimney and out again is a summary in itself. The entrance is the symbolic sexual act, and the exit the birth. The house is the uterus, the chimney the vagina (remember that the fetus is placed upside down).

The Yule traditions, are *talking*, we often can find the goat (Pan, adrenaline) to burn or destroy after Yule, but he is necessary at birth. It sometimes takes the form of a disguised man or woman, with a goatee mask, which frightens children on Yule Eve, or the figure of *Father-Whipper*.

Santa Claus' entrance and exit is totally secret, it must be done in privacy, intimacy. Often we put cakes for him at the fireplace and we receive candies from him.

The Christmas/Yule log (the traditional Yule cake in France), originally was a large log (placenta), which was sprinkled with wine (blood), and honey and we so let it burn until midnight (12, a solar year, the time of this ritual). Before putting it in the fire (birth), the last bride threw a small bag with coins (gold, knowledge), and the one who caught it had to touch the log with it (the placenta) before taking it home. This is the connection of the placenta (and amniotic bag) with knowledge, memory, and of course today food, since it is also a cake.

At Yule Eve and Yule day, the children were given a sip of alcohol (I do not recommend it, I prefer hot wine, and then hot honeyed milk, with the same symbols), symbol of body fluids (blood, then milk). They had to drink without using their hands (yes, like at Christian mass...), like fetuses and babies, who do not know how to use them.

Before Yule, we also went around the house with a branch of the Yule tree (ideally a branch of yew), when it had just been put in the house (the uterus): this to emphasize the limit (the walls) of the amniotic bag (part of the placenta, as the branch is part of the tree) and the uterus. *The hat trick*, in a way.

For my part, I will have taken in the tree forty days (forty weeks of pregnancies) before Yule, but if you do that it is not sure it will still have all its leaves at the Yule Eve. I advise then to take it in thirteen or twelve days (thirteen or twelve months, according to one or the other the calendar: the time of the ritual), or nine or ten days (months of pregnancy, always following one or the other calendar) before, or four weeks (as forty symbolic days) before Yule, as symbolize the four candles of Advent.

There is, in fact, no specific date for the entrance of the tree in the house (the uterus).

Yule Day, in fact, we should take it out (birth), but it is so hard then to get rid of it...

On the other hand, in the tradition, clawed animals must be outside on Yule Day, especially cats. You understand then that the placenta must come off, otherwise there will be hemorrhage and death of the mother.

From the burned Yule log, we kept a few pieces of charcoal, which was supposed to protect against diseases, and help to heal (like the truly magical powers of umbilical cord blood, capable of producing stem cells).

We see here the symbol of the piece of cord remained on the belly of the newborn. Eating the log (traditional Yule cake) is totally right with the meaning of this symbol, before Yule Day, on Yule Eve, and even after on Yule Day (remember that all mammals eat the placenta after birth...).

Santa Claus

The current image of Santa, contrary to modern legend, is not a creation of the company Coca Cola (which was attacked for its use as a merchandising tool after the Second World War). This one used a more or less local representation of Santa Claus for its advertising and thus globalized it. This representation, in red and white is quite right. Santa Claus brings together all the symbols: the blood red, and the snow white, the umbilical cord-beard, the water pocket cap, the water pocket hood, the ancestor's old age and the transmission, the sweets , children, sled, reindeer or deer ...

Santa Claus is *Heimdallr (HaimadalþaR)*, in Nordic mythology, Heimdallr is *the pole of the world, the center of the world, the world tree, the support of the world*, like the famous Irminsûl (*Varg Vikernes, Régis Boyer*). This reflects all that I explained above. The gravitational force is the center of the world, it is the tree that supports the world or the pillar of the world, it is where the roots are, it is what bears us, it is also Atlas, it is also Irminsûl ("great column" or "powerful column"), the pillar of Þórr, the pillar of the world, the tree of the world, Yggdrasill, the one who maintains the sky.

And yet there is no center of the world, not in the sense we understand it in the rules of geometry we know. But does geometry really take infinity into account? How could there be a center to infinity? A specific place for this pillar?

As I explained at the beginning of this book, it is not surprising, because there is no sphere strictly speaking, remember the number Pi, *this sphere is exploded, because of time. It has a center: it is gravitation,* it is only *present,* but it is quartered, in human time, because of human perspective.

Yggdrasill

The Yggdrasill tree, support of the world, as Irminsûl, or the column in the myth of Atlantis, or the pole at the Indra Jatra festival in Nepal) serves the nine worlds in Norse mythology. This is the nine months of pregnancy. Remember that time is described geographically, because, like geographical displacement, it is a movement.

*Destruction of Irminsûl by Charlemagne, symbolizing the
implantation of Christianity in France.*

Ancient symbol of Irminsûl (etymology: "big or powerful column")

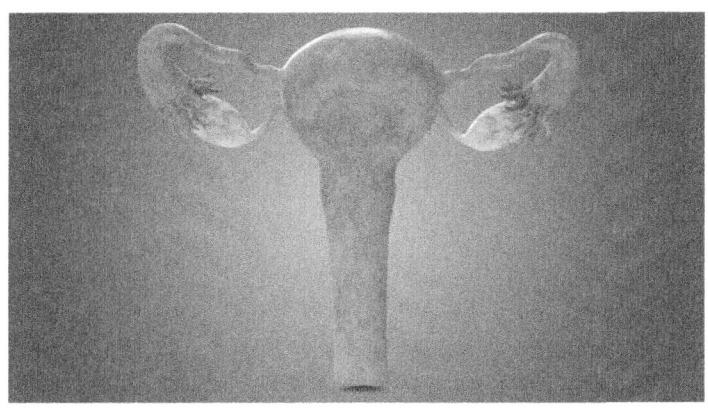

Female reproductive system

Irminsûl is an ash tree, ash is a protective tree of the uterus in herbal medicine. It works against hypertrophy of the uterus after childbirth, congestion of the uterus, and uterine prolapse.

And that's good, because you know that the Greek name for Heimdallr is Cronos... (Varg Vikernes, *Sorcery and Religion in Ancient Scandinavia*).

Rodolphe de Fulda, a monk, reports in the chapter 3 of his hagiography *De miraculis sancti Alexandri*:

Truncum quoque ligni non parvae magnitudinis in altum erectum sub divo colebant, patria eum lingua Irminsul appellantes, quod Latine dicitur universalis columna, quasi sustinens omnia.

There was also a tree trunk of unusual size, vertically erected, that they (the Saxons) worshiped in the outside, and which they called in their language "Irminsûl", which means in Latin "pillar of the world", as if it supported all things.

Of course it supports everything. How could we forget something so obvious, before seeming to rediscover it with modern science? Gravitation is the driving force, the essential force of our world, and it is intrinsically linked to time and life, to human time, or living time. It is the center of the world. As this symbolic tree is related to time, it has often been a yew, because the yew is the tree that lives the longest, and it always seems frozen in the present time, because it grows very slowly.

It is often said that our ancestors were afraid of the sky falling on their heads, and that is not totally wrong. Of course, it's greatly simplified. It is a way of saying that life stops, they come out of human time, they pass into another dimension.

Irminsûl, the pillar of the world, the gravitational force, is also the hammer of Þórr. Þórr's hammer: Mjöllnir, means *"the crusher"*, and is what brings about the lightning in the sky (Þórr means "thunderer") and it designates both this phenomenon, the heart, and the "crushing" gravitation (these three phenomena are related, the lightning being provoked by the gravitational force and its consequences in the clouds, and the heart being what keeps upright, what literally carries us).

Þá gaf hann Þór hamarinn ok sagði, at hann myndi mega ljósta svá stórt sem hann vildi, hvat sem fyrir væri, at eigi myndi hamarrinn bila, ok ef hann yrpi honum til, þá myndi hann aldri missa ok aldri fljúga svá langt, at eigi myndi hann sækja heim hönd, ok ef þat vildi, þá var hann svá lítill, at hafa mátti serk sér. En þat var lýi á, ar forskeftit var heldr skammt.

Then he gave the hammer to Þórr, and said that Þórr might smite as hard as he desired, whatsoever might be before him, and the hammer would not fail; and if he threw it at anything, it would never miss, and never fly so far as not to return to his hand; and if he desired, he might keep it in his pouch, it was so small; but indeed it was a flaw in the hammer that the fore-haft was somewhat short.

Skáldskaparmál, chapter 5

Þórr's hammer must also be brought closer to the vital (electrical) impulse that puts a body alive, the one that makes the heart beat (adrenaline, Pan).

It is well known today, while we revive hearts extinguished with the help of electrical impulses, this impulse could be at the origin of all life. Not a big, strong and powerful electricity as we know it today, but a small force, a tiny invisible electric force.

In any case, Mjöllnir is the ax, the symbol is exactly the same, the one that kills the tree, like Castor. Several myths relate Þórr's battles with snakes: like when he kills Jörmungandr, the Miðgarðr worm. Jörmungandr, from proto-Nordic *ErmunagandaR, meaning "the tremendous staff", "animated staff", "animated great cattle", "animated proto-ox". (Varg Vikernes, *Sorcery and Religion in Ancient Scandinavia*).

Note that Perun (the Slavic name for Þórr) has an axe, instead of a hammer.

Mjöllnir is therefore the heart, and symbolically the heart of stone waiting to be revived: the biface of the Stone Age (it is said that the hammer has a very short handle...), heart-shaped, often placed on the chest of the dead in the grave, since the Neanderthal, but always shown in books in reverse of its symbolic function: upside down, feet in the air. The biface, a multi-tool in Stone Age, indispensable to man, devoid of weapons and sharp teeth, is also the symbol of his heart.

Like the heart, it strikes; and later also the ax, the true one, or all the symbolic axes also, this one strikes, strikes, and strikes again the tree, so that it gives its energy.

Note that in that Stone Age (before a certain period which itself is not really defined), they did not have any axes. They probably picked up the dead wood for the fire, and that was enough.

Tree cutting is newer.

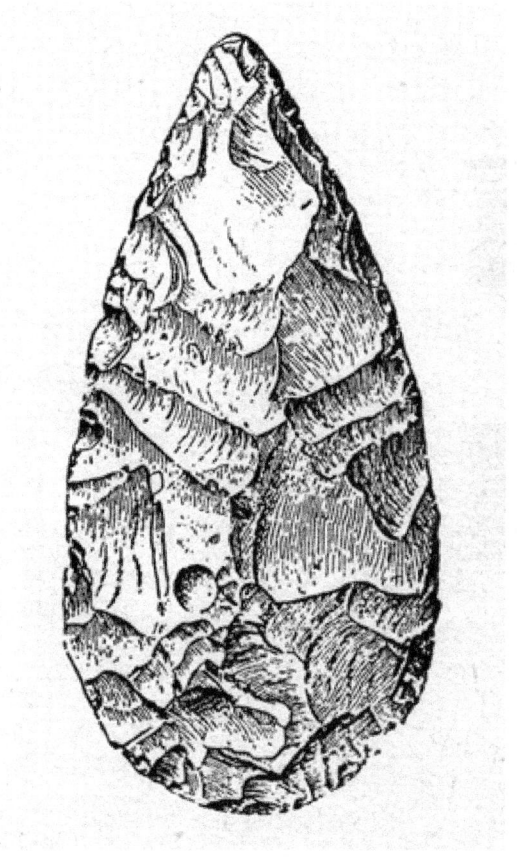

Acheulean Biface

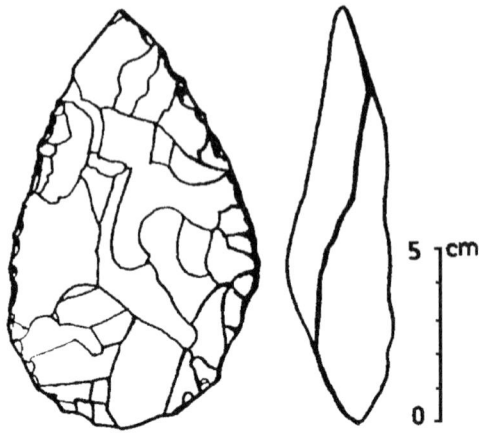

Heart-shaped biface

Regarding the biface representing the heart, I must mention the one who was named "Excalibur" (his name is particularly well chosen), which is half red; but not only...

Near Stonehenge, and I think the place was chosen for this reason, there is a river (the Avon River) in which the objects, and especially the stones, turn red. This is linked to the presence of algae (Hildenbrandia rivularis) and a particularly warm water for the region, if we dip them for a moment in the water, and then they come out, they turn pink red.

What an interesting symbol to image a heart of stone that comes to life... in water (the amniotic fluid)!

Cronos (Greek) is Saturn (Roman) and Toth and Maat (Egyptian). Saturn is the feast of Saturnalia. This celebration was held around the winter solstice, from December 17th to 24th (seven days), then on December 25th with the *Dies Natalis Solis Invicti "the birth day of Sol Invictus"*. Sol Invictus being the same god as Mithra, whom we have already mentioned.

During the Saturnalia, the hierarchical order is temporarily reversed. Slaves are masters. We offer small gifts. It is generally accepted that Saturnalia have been partly inspired by religious or traditional festivals:
- The Christian Christmas day takes up the symbol of the winter solstice, the Sol invictus theme (the undefeated sun).
- The kings' cake, which would crown the "king" of the festival.
- Carnival disguises and processions.

Slaves were similar to children under the Roman Empire, and the fact that they enjoyed an apparent and temporary freedom during these festivities seems to indicate that children were considered differently during this period. They are no longer children, but personalities with many lives behind. It is not surprising that they are looked at in another way. Suddenly a door opens. The child has recovered the head of the ancestor and the knowledge of past lives, he is no longer a seven years old creature, he is a person, he gets a name (see Perceval), he was born, he is considered.

So why the gifts?

Have you ever wondered why you pack gifts for your children? In the Yule, but also at birthdays? Birthday parties are also very interesting. The birthday cake represents the placenta, and the candles the umbilical cord, whose fire (blood) is cut by the child when he blows on the candle. This is just a reminder of the rebirth each year. Here again we find the same ritual, everyone repeats it mechanically, without asking any question about its meaning.

But then why do you pack the gifts? Because they are buried. They are hidden, hidden with the dead, in the grave. But also in the amniotic bag, in the womb. You know, they always say that the dead were buried with personal effects because at that time, our ancestor believed they were going to need them in the afterlife. It's both totally false and laughable, and true.

Since Christian times, our Pagan ancestors have been systematically seen as idiots. But at the same time, this explanation is not absolutely false. We must see at *The Book of the Dead* of ancient Egypt, which is supposed to help the dead find the way into the afterlife, and which, in my opinion, tells the story of the arrival of the child who is going to fetch the ancestor (See the movie *ForeBears*, by Varg Vikernes and myself).

These explanations are true, if the afterlife is the other life, but the other real life, not that of an imaginary and paradisiac world, but the life of the child who finds himself and the ancestor who is reborn. So yes, in this case it's just, these belongings are for him in the afterlife, in his new life.

It is therefore normal for him to come in search for them, to open them, to dig them up. These "gifts" will allow him to remember his past life, to remember, as for the modern amnesic I described at the beginning of the book.

They are deposited with the allegoric birth, today symbolically by a being who represents the totality of this ritual: the famous Santa Claus, at the same time ancestor, placenta, pillar of the world, bear, dwarf, fetus. It is customary to give him honey cakes or other food stuff, because like the bear he is very gluttonous, and because, if you feed the she-bear, she will feed you.

He is the placenta, the one who devours to give food, and to give knowledge. In the womb (in the tomb, in the cave, in the house), he transmits the gifts, that is to say his own personal belongings, since he is the ancestor, but he transmits them to himself, as a child. A gift is also called a present. A very... obvious word, you will agree. It is the past belongings coming back to... *present*.

These belongings are indeed what bring memories back to the present, the past to the present. With them, it becomes possible to remember. Remember amnesia. Gifts, like gold, are knowledge because they make reminiscence possible: the remembrance of a memory, even it is not always recognized as such. The Platonists thus believed that almost all the knowledge we acquire are only reminiscences of what we knew before our birth.

You see, I am not lying to you. So what does Plato say in his *Allegory of the cave*? He says, as usual, much more than it seems. It tells the remains of an extremely ancient ritual.

The analogy of the belly or the womb with the tomb or the cave is very clear. The apposition of the fetal hands inside the womb is too, it is as old as the beginnings of writing. From the "positive" and "negative" hands in caves in Stone Age. It is also shown that these hands are small, probably, they said, women's or adolescents' hands. *Maybe seven or eight years old children?*

As the age of the only two footprints found in ornate caves (*Pech Merle, France* and *Chauvet Pont d'Arc, France*). It has been demonstrated that they belonged to children of about seven or eight years. It is very delicate to measure a painted hand affixed against an irregular stone wall. But there is something else.

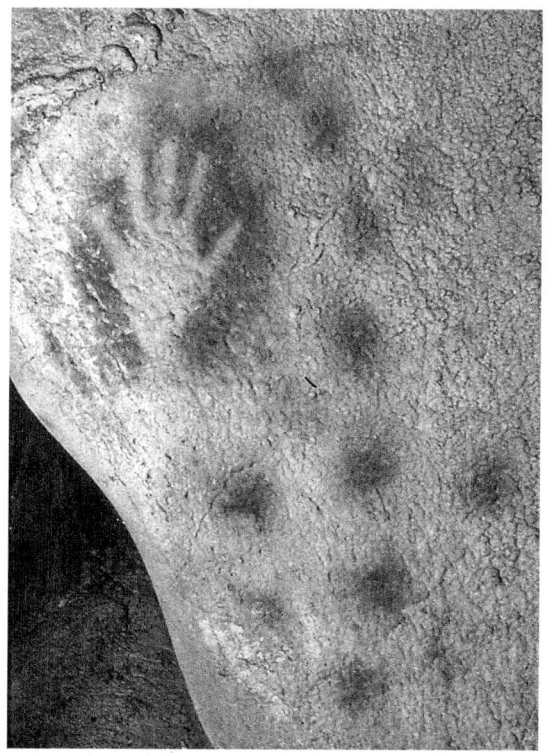

Negative hand, Pech-Merle cave, -20,000, France

If you know about the symbol of the labyrinth, you surely know about the Trojan labyrinth symbol (also called "Cretan labyrinth")? The one supposed to represent, in one way or another, the city of Troy, which is found in all Europe, from Greece to Scandinavia.

Cretan or Trojan Labyrinth

Moreover *Ásgarðr, the kingdom of the gods* in Norse mythology is called *Troy* too. This is the same mythical city. Strange? Strange also, that the mother of Romulus and Remus, *Rhea Silvia,* is also called *Ilia, "the Trojan".* Very strange, this Ilia, and this mythical city presents *everywhere.*

Romulus and Remus

The two mythical twins Romulus and Remus are an excellent image of our history. Their mother is Rhea Silvia, vestal, therefore the "virgin", the egg, and their adoptive mother (understand the symbolic belly, the symbolic uterus, the bear) is a wolf or a prostitute (understand: the symbolic female genital and reproductive system). They are delivered to the wolf by her husband. They are two, like Castor and Pollux, because there is the fetus (Romulus) and the placenta (Remus), killed by his own brother.

This labyrinth, you know it very well, you have it on your fingers. Yes, it's the famous modern biometric ID card. It's a kind of map. Unique to each person, it is even unique to each twin. It is thought that it is drawn by amniotic fluid, or in other words the ambrosia. The fingerprint, or rather *the dermatoglyph* (literally *"skin carvings"*), the fingerprint being its representation, like the famous positive and negative hands. Is it the very symbol of individuality, the map of your journey in the afterlife.

You may not believe me if I tell you that some cave-tombs (dolmens or mounds) are filled with them. You will not believe me because no one has presented it to you as well. Scholars working on History and especially Prehistory, are not often inclined to talk about continuity between so remote periods. And yet...

Is it not the same symbol? Is it not the same message in the ornate caves (positive and negative hands), and in the tumulus of Gavrinis (France) covered by, what I wish to call, with all my will, *"dermatoglyphs"*? But also today, with our famous and in fact very little modern, *"biometrics"*? The identification of people has always been a human concern. Why can't we see the similarity of these symbols?

The fetus puts his hands on the wall of the uterus and marks his passage, with these, and with his *dermatoglyphs*, which leave unique prints, evidence of his subjectivity.

These dermatoglyphs are also seen as a map, as they are today (a map of DNA, identity, and so of what makes your life, a map of *the time spent as yourself*): They are the famous symbol of the labyrinth and the city of Troy, which will be discussed later. How can one describe Gavrinis' obvious engravings as *"bizarre drawings"*? (Prosper Mérimée, *Notes de voyage dans l'ouest de la France*, 1836), how can one be so blind?

Engraved walls in the cairn of Gavrinis, Brittany, France

The cairns and other dolmens or tumulus are clearly an image of the uterus, with their long corridor (vagina) and their round or triangular "burial chamber". Often, there is even the cervix, a small circle dug in the stone, to enter the funeral chamber.

A dolmen in Caucasus mountain

A dolmen in Adygea, Russia

Megalithic tomb near Vozrozhdenie village and Gelendzhik town. Krasnodar Krai. Russia

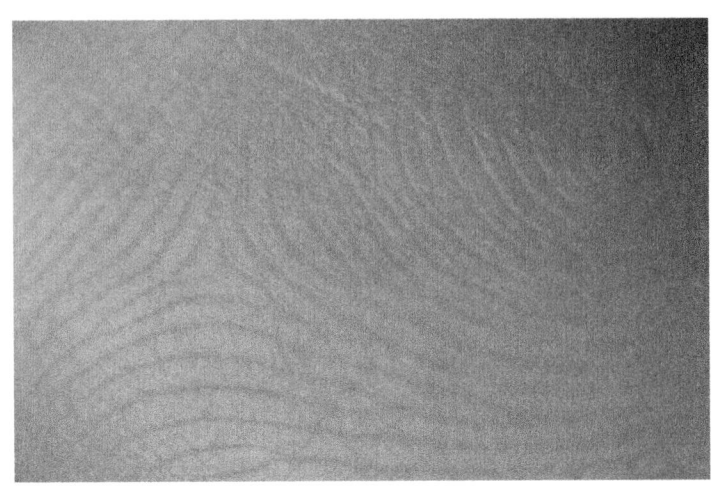

*Dermatoglyph (etymologically "skin carvings")
on a human finger*

Engraved walls in the cairn of Gavrinis, Brittany, France

You must know that the first animal to engrave on the rock walls in the caves is not the man, but the bear, after the period of hibernation, probably to sharpen its claws. Traces of bear scratches are found in several decorated caves, above, below and alongside many human engravings or paintings (notably *Bara-Bahau Cave* in France, and *Rouffignac Cave* in France, where the man seems to have more or less imitated the bear, with digital traces).

This symbol, found in several ornate caves, is for me a schematized bear print. Note that the bear paws are (with some imagination) very close to those of men:

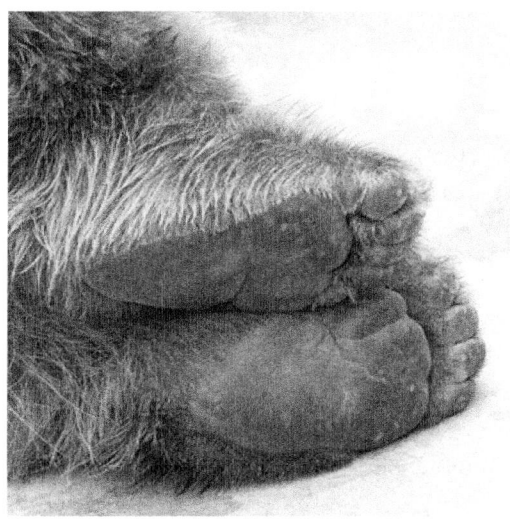

Bear feet

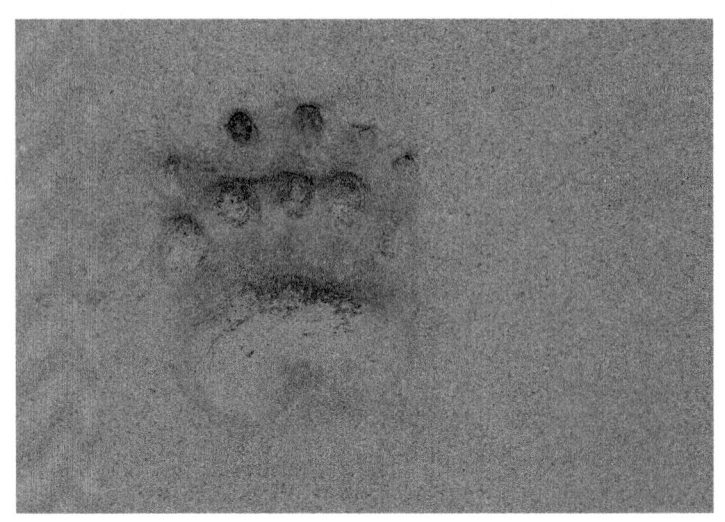

Bear footprint (front leg)

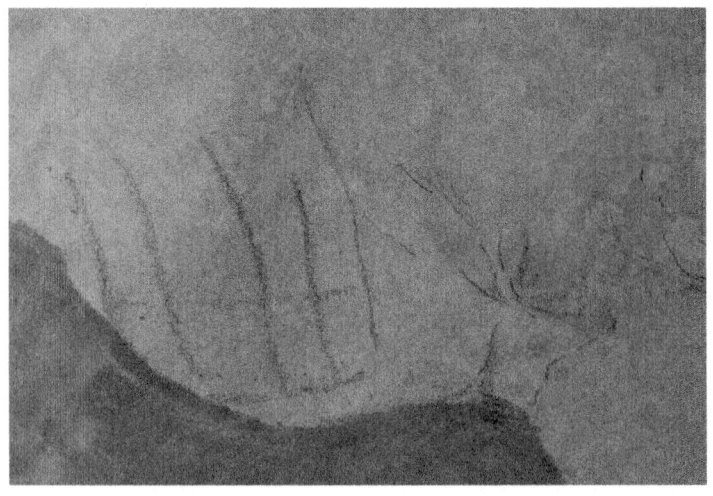

Artistic interpretation, Lascaux

The analogy between the house and the uterus is also very clear. The chimney being this famous corridor: the vagina; the house: the uterus or the funerary chamber. The Yule tree is brought inside, it too is an obvious representation of the placenta. *The tree of Life*. It is decorated in red (blood) or golden (light) with garlands, an image of the umbilical cord; balls, an image of the bloody fruit, or bloody food; and light (today electric, before nutshells with oil), an image of the flowing life, the blood, the energy from the sun.

As previously reported, the Yule tree is, even today, sometimes decorated with reindeer and deer, with dwarves, but also, more strangely, with bears and bear cubs. The bear is an unofficial symbol of Yule. As if it were anchored in the collective memory. Bears with hats, humanized bears, automaton bears. Strangely, in fact, the bear seems to designate Yule without anyone being able to explain why or how.

But wait. Why do we put shoes, or a sock, under the tree? Now you must remember the boots of seven leagues, and the slipper of Cinderella. Why do you tell your children to put their shoes (a pair, or just one) under the Yule tree?

And if they asked you, what would you tell them? No doubt that Santa Claus must be able to know where they are. And you will be right. *The shoe is the human body alive*. It is the legs standing, so in working condition. Once again, remember the tomb of *Le Regourdou (France)*, a 70,000 years old Neanderthal tomb. Nothing has changed, you always do the same, and 2,000 years of Christianity have failed to erase so old traditions.

It is not the only tomb to present these characteristics, but its age makes it particularly interesting. In addition to the missing head, the two legs of the dead were missing. They were replaced by bear legs. Bear, gravitation, do you remember? The legs, the feet are those who bears. But to do that, they must be vertical, go a little against the gravitational force, they are then able to carry themselves, thanks to the beating heart and flowing blood. The blood brings oxygen, so the breath. And blood is created with oxygen in the bone itself, in the marrow. It is the symbol of the flute, the bone flute.

The oldest flute is the 45,000-year-old Neanderthal flute from *Divje Babe (Slovenia)*. It is made in a cave bear cub's leg. Well.

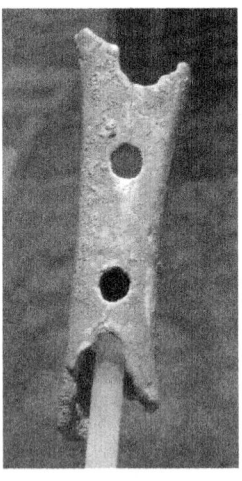

Neanderthal flute from Divje Babe, Slovenia, -45,000 years

What do we do in this bone? We blow. By blowing we are transforming that blow into something else, in this case music, blood. Music is also the language of birds, angels... The bird, remember, is the allegory of the dead, the fetus, the ancestor, the placenta. It is this little being who blows like the wind and in the wind, *whistles with the wind*, and speaks a language that we know (music) without really understanding it. In fact, *we feel it.*

The shins, the femurs, the legs are the ones who carry the life, who carry the dead therefore. It is about what makes him progress in human time, blood, as music, which can only exist with time. They move so fast because this speed is compared to the dead who does not move in time (he is in the present, in Eternity), when, on the contrary, the human time moves. Rather than a geographical displacement, it is a displacement in time that is often described, but these boots of seven leagues, that is to say, this seven-year-old body (or finished body, weaned body, individual body) is the life vehicle we were talking about at the beginning of the book.

You place your shoes under the tree so that the ancestor (yourself) can slip in (slip into your body, in other words) accompanied by gifts (your personal belongings, your knowledge) buried with him (with you). It is not seven leagues geographically speaking, but seven leagues temporally speaking, where the year is the league, the unit of measure. In mythology, it is almost always the case, and it is essential to be able to understand all these stories.

Of course the shoe or boot fits the wearer's foot, or suits him perfectly (like that of *Cinderella*) because the wearer is him, it is his shoe, his body. The body recognizes the soul, and the soul recognizes the body. Your body is adapted to you? You don't even ask yourself this question, because it's obvious.

Tom Thumb takes the boots of the (now really dead) ancestor.

Here it is the fetus who takes the boots from the ancestor. Do not forget that the two are the same person. It is about a transmission.

Of course, it is the same symbol in the description of Þórr's chariot, pulled by two goats named *Tanngrisnir* and *Tanngnjostr* (*"Grinding teeth"* and *"Sparkling teeth"*, the so-called *permanent teeth*, are the symbol of the ancestor who takes possession of the/his seven-year-old weaned body). These goats could be eaten every day, and they would come back to life the next day if their leg bones were not broken.

The chariot is this mysterious vehicle that carries in life (human time) that I mentioned at the beginning. It is also and always the gravitational chariot (the placenta, the great bear). As you have understood, these two analogies are the same, each time it is about to be worn, whether by the placenta, by the mother, by Earth or universal gravitation, or by the legs, the heart, the blood. This gravitational force is closely related to human time, it is its symptom.

It is on the Yule morning this birth takes place, when the gifts are deposited at the foot of the tree, in the shoes. It is the birth of the ancestor in his new weaned body: the knowledge that enters the body, *the reminiscence.*

Reincarnation.

This re-birth, it may surprise you, it is also the one which is told in *the Iliad*, the story of the Trojan War. It's the reincarnation of Achilles we are there talking about. With our modern words, and for simplicity, because it may take a whole book to analyze this war, we could say that Achilles (*"without lips": the one who has never approached the lips of a breast: the fetus, see Apollodorus previously cited.*) and his ancestor Patroclus (*"the glory of the father"*) is the one who lives again, Hector (*from the ancient Greek Ἕκτωρ, and before ἔχω, Héktôr, from * ϝεχέτω, the Indo-European common * weǵʰ- "drive", "move"*) being the boots, the vehicle...

The Trojan Hector plays the role of the placenta-ancestor, the one whom, at this moment of the story, one must fight (he is by the way hit in his, in other words: slaughtered, and hung up and dragged after the chariot of Achilles, the newly born fetus... What an image for the umbilical cord and its placenta!). Helen (*"sun burst"!*) is, of course, life, preserved in Troy (*the womb*), and returned, given to Achilles-Patroclus. The others are mainly doubles of the main characters (*Briseis*, the companion of Achilles, for *Helen*), or others. *This story is as old as the world, if I may say so.* Probably this is the reason why *Ásgarðr*, in Norse mythology, is also called *"Troy"*, probably that is why the Trojan labyrinth is found throughout Europe. The story is close to the mythical war between Atlanteans and Greeks (see the story of *Atlantis*, in *the Critias*, by Plato: remember, the famous flood is none other than the rupture of the amniotic bag, during the birth).

By the way, Troy simply does not have any etymology. Trojan (or Troy) comes from *Troy, tros*, or any nearby word simply designating the same thing: *the city of Troy*. For me, this means that this name, this word, this city, or this way to designate the womb (the fortified city) is extremely old.

For my part, I bring this name closer to the number three (*trois* in French, pronounced exactly like the name of the city), quite simply, a number whose name is almost identical in all the European languages (from the common Indo-European * *tréyes*).

In the written history, in the Iliad, the signs, the proofs, are innumerable. Sometimes they are very discrete details, but completely incoherent if one does not understand the story as it should be, and they are completely and wildly ignored by the classical analyzers.

Oddly enough, *Hector (moving, the chariot)* fights *Achilles (the fetus)* with *Patroclus' armor (the glory of the father, Mímir, the memory)*, taken from *Patrocles (the glory of the father)* that he has himself killed. This same armor was in fact that of *Achilles (the fetus, the seven years old child)*, I want to say "his old skin", "his old body", which he had lent to *Patrocle (the glory of the father)* his older friend, to go fight the Trojans (enter the ritual of reincarnation and his three symbolic pregnancies).

As I told you, Achilles seizes the remains of his enemy Hector whom he attaches to his chariot by the tendons of the ankles and he drags him to the Greek ships.

You will have recognized the placenta-cord, hanging to the body of the fetus Achilles, who, for the birth-fight with the placenta-Hector was decked out with a brand new armor (body) created by the gods, its old being worn by Hector, stolen from the remains of Patroclus.

The two armor being made in bronze, *i. e.* reddish, or *"vermilion"* to quote Perceval and refer you to the famous *"vermeil knight"* or *"red knight"* from which Perceval desires to possess the armor.

And yet this is only the end of this long poem. All along you had been made aware of the real reason for this war, and its true meaning.

Besides, I must tell you, *the famous Achilles heel is the body of course. This is the weakness of the soul, the mortal side of the body.* Once again, the foot, the leg, represents the body. Sometimes it's the hand, the glove.

Remember the extract of the story I quoted before:

We were ranged round about a fountain offering hecatombs to the gods upon their holy altars, and there was a fine plane-tree from beneath which there welled a stream of pure water. Then we saw a sign ; for Zeus sent a fearful serpent out of the ground, with blood-red stains upon its back,

and it darted from under the altar on to the plane-
tree. Now there was a brood of young sparrows,
quite small, upon the topmost bough, peeping out
from under the leaves, eight in all, and their mother
that hatched them made nine. The serpent ate the
poor cheeping things,

while the old bird flew about lamenting her little
ones; but the serpent threw his coils about her and
caught her by the wing as she was screaming. Then,
when he had eaten both the sparrow and her young,
the god who had sent him made him become a sign;
for the son of scheming Kronos turned him into
stone,

and we stood there wondering at that which had
come to pass. Seeing, then, that such a fearful
portent had broken in upon our hecatombs, Kalkhas
forthwith declared to us the oracles of heaven.
'Why, Achaeans,' said he, 'are you thus speechless?
Zeus has sent us this sign,

long in coming, and long ere it be fulfilled, though
its fame [kleos] shall last for ever. As the serpent ate
the eight fledglings and the sparrow that hatched
them, which makes nine, so shall we fight nine
years at Troy, but in the tenth shall take the town.'

Homer, *The Iliad*

Why, *while this is explicitly stated*, why has this text
not been understood? Has the world been muzzled by
(only) 2,000 years of Christianity?

In this detail, in this extract from the Iliad, absolutely all the meaning of the text is explained. All is said. The Greeks, always described as dumb and with hairy heads (the newborns, therefore, unlike the Trojans who are always described *screaming*) fought for nine years (nine months) and take Troy and Helen (life) in the tenth year. So what kind of proofs is still needed?

It is even talked about the risk of being changed into stone by the placenta. And that is physically true, I remind you, if a fetus stays too long inside the womb (*"the son of Kronos"* means of course *time,* Kronos means "time"), the placenta calcifies, and also changes the fetus into a stone fetus, *a lithopedion,* which can then remain several years or decades in the womb of his mother.

There are many other details, which we do not usually see, but which are nevertheless there to explain the meaning of the Trojan War:

There is of course the shield of *Ajax* (*etymology: "relative of the deceased"*!), with the seven bull skins, plus a bronze (red) blade.

There are some recurring metaphors:

"As long as the warm blood gushed from his wound, Agamemnon kept on attacking with spear and sword and huge rocks. But when the wound started to dry and the blood hardened, sharp pains came over him, just like the pains that stab a woman in labour, sent by the spirits of childbirth, the daughters of Hera in charge of those violent pangs. "

(...)

" *While they were stripping from these their shining arms, meanwhile the youths that followed with Polydamas and Hector, even they that were most in number and bravest, and that most were fain to break through the wall and burn the ships with fire, these still tarried in doubt, as they stood by the trench.* **For a bird had come upon them, as they were eager to cross over, an eagle of lofty flight, skirting the host on the left, and in its talons it bore a blood-red, monstrous snake, still alive as if struggling, nor was it yet forgetful of combat, it writhed backward, and smote him that held it on the breast beside the neck, till the eagle, stung with pain, cast it from him to the ground, and let it fall in the midst of the throng, and himself with a loud cry sped away down the blasts of the wind. And the Trojans shuddered when they saw the writhing snake lying in the midst of them, a portent of Zeus that beareth the aegis.**

Then verily Polydamas drew near, and spake to bold Hector: "Hector, ever dost thou rebuke me in the gatherings of the folk, though I give good counsel, since it were indeed unseemly that a man of the people should speak contrariwise to thee, be it in council or in war, but he should ever increase thy might; yet now will I speak even as seemeth to me to be best. Let us not go forward to fight with the Danaans for the ships.

For thus, methinks, will the issue be, seeing that in sooth this bird has come upon the Trojans, as they were eager to cross over, an eagle of lofty flight, skirting the host on the left, bearing in his talons a blood-red, monstrous snake, still living, yet straightway let it fall before he reached his own nest, neither finished he his course, to bring and give it to his little ones—even so shall we, though we break the gates and the wall of the Achaeans by our great might, and the Achaeans give way, come back over the selfsame road from the ships in disarray; for many of the Trojans shall we leave behind, whom the Achaeans shall slay with the bronze in defense of the ships. On this wise would a soothsayer interpret, one that in his mind had clear knowledge of omens, and to whom the folk gave ear."

Homer, The Iliad

A small stop to detail the etymologies of Hector and Helen:

Hector: From ἕκτωρ, Héktôr, "further ahead", from ancient Greek ἔχω: ékhô: "to bear".

*(Verb 1) From common Indo-European * seǵʰ- ("to have", "to possess")*

*(Verb 2) From * ϝεχέτω, from the common Indo-European * weǵʰ- ('to drive', 'to move')*

ἔχω, ekhô, verb:

Attached to.
To seize, to seize, to take.
Hold back.
Keep firm, contain, maintain.
To repress, to stop.
Depend on.
Stand back.

Weird, when Hector is, I believe, the representation of the ancestor-placenta-cord, that his very name means *"to attach to"*, *"to retain"*, *"to maintain"*, *"to depend on"*, or even *"to stand back"*. Isn't it? Remember the witch-stepmother in the tale of *Rapunzel*.

Helen: from Greek hêlê, probably "sun shine", "sun burst".

Helen is the virgin, she represents the life to take. Life is always *the energy of the sun*. We can add that it is linked to the exit of the womb, where the fetus finally sees "the sun shine".

Briseis, with name from unknown origin, is the avatar of Helen, she also represents, as a virgin, the fetus, the life. She is given to and taken from Achilles (death) who is in love with her, then she is proposed to him again to convince him to go fight the Trojans (be born) with the other Greeks.

Briseis with beautiful cheeks, as she is called, means that she holds the blood in her (rosy cheeks), life. Again, it is actually not a virgin in the modern sense, but the symbol of a baby, a little girl, do not we often say about babies that they have "beautiful cheeks"? There is the same image in the tale of Perceval, when he longs for *Blanchefleur*, his companion, and remembers her (life), when he sees drops of blood falling in the snow: this blood in the snow reminds him of the red on the white... of Blanchefleur's cheeks.

EPILOGUE

At Yule, under the protection of the she-bear, carried by gravity and at the same time able to challenge her, because he is *alive*, at Yule, the ancestor is reborn in the body of a young child of about seven years. He is reborn physically through the adult teeth or permanent teeth, genetically and psychologically. This child acquires a personality, or rather an identity, and a name. He is no longer a child, he is the ancestor and will be recognized as such, especially through his name and the objects and belongings (gold: knowledge...) that are given to him or that he himself seek in what is considered as his own grave.

As with the modern treatment of amnesia, these objects and belongings (but also the trees that can see everything around them and live for thousands of years, especially the yew planted on the tomb of the dead) will help to remember his past life (lives), whose memories are part of his genetic heritage (see recent studies showing the modification of the living's DNA and the integration of personal memories to the genetic heritage given to children and descendants). Superstition! Maybe you will believe that. And yet. It is said that nearly all Frenchmen, French over several generations, are descendants of Charlemagne.

Obviously this is an example. You are not only descendants of *Charlemagne*, but also of all the Frenchmen of that time. If we go back further, it will involve even more people, more Europeans as a whole. So the burial under this 4000 years old dolmen contains... *you*.

Yes in a way, it's really you, and probably also, you are today as much German, English... This bronze sword in a museum? It's yours. It's *really* yours.

But that goes further, of course. The Neanderthal tomb of *Le Regourdou (France, -70,000 years)* contains a body that is that of all Europeans, and even more, probably. So who is it? *It's you.* We forget that today, when we visit historical sites or museums, we look at bones like those of other individuals, and yet, genetically speaking, they are *yours.* However, the identity seems to be attached to a person, an individual (remember: *individual* means *who is indivisible*). This tradition, this ritual of reincarnation is as old as the world seems to demonstrate it. Why ? What if there were some "memory genes"? A genetic inheritance that would tend to reform itself, after, sometimes, thousands of years? At least partly? What if love attraction held hidden secrets in it, as if genes from identical memories were attracting themselves, in order to reform an individual? So you could be carrying memory genes without having access to them yourself. It would take two identical for them to be activated.

From the point of view of Nature (and with a modern look), which always seems to be energy-efficient, this is quite conceivable, in order to avoid a possible extinction by awakening some knowledge acquired thousands of years ago, then forgotten because it was possibly unnecessary for a moment. In this way intelligence and adaptability can be partly a reminiscence of past discoveries and knowledge.

Imagine that a solar storm deprives the world of electrical energy overnight, which, from a physical and even a statistical point of view, is possible. Almost all of what you have learned for your "survival" in the modern world is dependent on electrical energy, which has assisted you throughout your life, and throughout the life of your parents. Are you going to die? Perhaps... But Nature has given you the keys to get out of it, as it has given to all living things. The dependency on learning in man is such that it can be dangerous, but it is a bit less if we are able to remember what we have acquired a thousand years, ten thousand years, or fifty thousand years ago. If you have never learned it, will you be able to light a fire, or if you are missing a tool, to cut a stone, as men have done for hundreds of thousands of years? Probably not. And yet, maybe so. You will call it intelligence, but it may be *reminiscence*, as Socrates suggested, or what is often called "instinct."

The baby at birth knows how to breathe "instinctively", and he knows how to suckle the breast "instinctively".

Perhaps these instincts are reminiscences, directly related to survival, and totally obvious. Perhaps this ability to print things in her genetic heritage is a way to create new instincts.

Our forebears believed in this transmission of individuality, which is called reincarnation. It was not just a banal superstition but a conclusion based on the observation of Nature and its functions and the way it works.

This observation, which revealed recurring patterns in Nature, allowed them to understand the role of the different elements that compose it, in an extremely astonishing way. Thus all energy comes from the sun, and all life acts as a brake on the dispersion of this energy, a way to preserve it. The tree, an obvious symbol of this energy "pump", was at the center of the science of our European ancestors. It was vital, as the placenta is vital to the fetus. The patterns of the tree, the pattern "ramifications" explained its role: like any branching, any ramification, this pattern suggests a flow, and often an exchange of "fluids" (streams, rivers and rivers, blood vessels and placenta, lightning).

Here it is a flow: that of light, through photosynthesis, from the sun to the ground, to the trunk; but also an exchange, since the tree transpires a lot of water so that this photosynthesis is possible (without water the leaves would burn or dry in the sun).

Paradoxically we know today that this water transpired in the sky itself attracts the rain towards the lands and the forests competing with the evaporation of the oceans.

The other side of the exchange is that of the streams and rivers that flow "dirty water" (the blood drained of oxygen) to the heart (the seas that beat, with the tides, with the help of gravity and the moon).

Of course, we must remember that there is another exchange too, gaseous this time, between oxygen and carbon dioxide.

With this energy pump, the tree feeds the entire Earth with solar energy, and with water and gas necessary for its survival it removes waste, as the placenta-cord offers blood to the fetus and cleans it. Plants are playing the same role. The energy of the sun is in a certain way offered to the animals (who themselves feed the plants by their droppings in particular).

The understanding of the analogy between the placenta-cord and the tree is essential to conceive the scope of the religion-science of our European ancestors. We must also understand that the biotope of the Native European man is forest, which explains its fair skin, which does not tolerate a too strong sun but is able to synthesize quickly, and with very little sun the vitamin D, essential to survival. In fact, the tree is elementary, primordial, offering man food, water, and oxygen, but also building materials, house and heating, fundamental for humans in Europe and in the Northern hemisphere. Indeed, the Native European man is built for the cold, but not necessarily the extreme cold, that the Inuit and Lapps tolerate better. On the other hand, the Native European man is tremendously adapted to the very weak sunshine in forest at our latitudes.

Another main factor required to understand the science of our ancestors, since Stone Age, is the consideration of the gravitational force. It is of course closely linked to the biomass, to the mass of the Earth, but also to so-called philosophical considerations. Indeed, this force is what carries the world *in time*, as an anchorage, a pillar, a trunk, a pole emerging from *Eternity*.

The planets, stars, and other masses of the universe are carried as small leaves by a single force.

To take up again the image of the only existing time, namely *the present, the instant*, represented by an infinite ball (the seed), and thus carried by itself, by its center of gravity; this one is found, in the human time (which is only a point of view), quartered in an infinite number of small scattered moments (the leaves) always carried by the same center (the trunk, emergence of the seed). All this is only an analogy, an image, but it is useful to understand it. The one who carries the world in mythology is *Atlas* and earlier this force was represented by a (she-)bear here in Europe, especially because the bear (whose etymology is identical to the verb *to bear*, and *arctos*, the bear, represents *the Arctic, the North Pole*, the force holding the Earth) is an obvious symbol of physical strength. The Great Bear was a female because it is the female who bears the cubs. The mother thus symbolically defies the gravitational force in the realm of the dead where it can no longer be defied alone, because life is that: the transmitted energy allows us to counter, at least a little, the gravitational force : *life* is indeed *getting out of the seed*, the "eternal ball", at least in the point of view of the human time.

This separation of the gravitational force in the human point of view is also symbolized by the imprint of the wheel (ball) and of course in mathematics by the number Pi. 3,14 ...

We understand the importance of the number three (Troy) in European culture, everything having to symbolically turn three times before having the speed to live (..., 141 592 653 589 793 ...). The force to turn three times is contained in the seed and always transmitted by *Pan, the adrenaline*. πῖ, pî is the first letter of the ancient Greek alphabet, the beginning of the story in fact, Pi gave the word periphery, but also "péripétie" in French, which means "adventure", "event".

In this regard, an additional anecdote will make you understand the importance of totemism in the releasing of adrenaline necessary for all life (sexual act, birth). I explained to you that natural childbirth required a loss of inhibitions, a deactivation of the rational brain. In other words, in certain cases it is necessary to know how to become an animal, to become your animal double.

In intimacy, during a childbirth for example, this is usually done naturally, under the impulse of a unique hormonal balance, a blend of oxytocin, endorphin and adrenaline. But if that was not possible, the witch midwives used herbal potions, among other things. In these well-controlled cases, and only in these rare cases, we accepted and desired the appearance of the self-totem or self-animal, self-bear (*beserk*: *"bear skin"*, which is traditionally called *"trance"*). This *apparition* is in fact rather *a disappearance* of the rational self. Alcohol plays the same role. *Michel Odent* explains that when he was director of the maternity in *Pithiviers*, in a double room a woman celebrated the birth of her child with *champagne*, while another had just started to come in labor.

The latter was offered champagne by the first and gave birth... immediately. The champagne rise to the brain very quickly, it disinhibits and, in this case, it helped the appearance of the totem animal of the woman in labor, her self-animal, and caused a rapid implementation of the ejection reflex of the fetus. Of course, the use of these substances is not recommended, for many reasons specific to Nature it is important that the hormonal balance comes naturally but it explains that they could be used by midwives (witches) in cases of difficult or seemingly impossible deliveries. The forceps of Stone Age.

We have seen through the phenomenon of "crystallization" in children, that they seem to identify with a hero. No doubt this ideal or real hero represents an externalization of their personality and their identity. Our ancestors interpreted this movement of self to the outside as the search for their lost identity through the amnesia of death. To awaken their memories, to find themselves, they had to reproduce the ritual of passage from death to life, a ritual in three parts, like three pregnancies, like the 3 of the number Pi, like Troy, to then be able to write the new life they will live (*"péripétie"* in French *"event"*, *"adventure"*: περιπετής), in what constitutes exactly the infinitude of this number, the number after the comma. This ritual lasted one year, divided into three symbolic pregnancies nested in each other. The three starts.

It took place at the loss of the first baby teeth (the bean in the Kings' cake), this loss marked the biological weaning of the child and therefore his living condition, his individuality, since he from then on was feed only with the elements of the outside world. It announced the arrival of the adult teeth, in other words the ancestor symbolically appeared physically in the child. Psychically this period, around seven years, is the arrival of the age of reason, which is characterized by an opening of the child on learning, and the loss of infantile selfishness necessary for his survival before seven years. The child becomes aware of the consequences of his actions, he becomes responsible, an adult in becoming, whereas he was not even an individual before, since he was dependent on the mother for his survival (and therefore not *"indivisible" without provoking his death*).

This ritual is probably older than the traces it left, beginning from -70,000 years ago, in the Neanderthal tomb of *Le Regourdou,* in France, throughout history until today, with still lasting traditions and classic tales still told to children. All the archaeological remains related to death in pre-Christian Europe, are related to this ritual, and all the remarkable sites such as decorated caves and later megaliths. The menhirs, meanwhile, present in large numbers in Brittany, are an image of dying men, who go down to the sea to the west of Europe, like the sun. They are *the fossilized presence of the ancestor*. A menhir is a standing man, a stone that says "I was there".

It really says so to archaeologists, because as some soil is added each year to the soil of the last year, we are able to know when they were laid, until they are completely covered. This descent into the sea to the West is, in my opinion, the reason why they are so common in Brittany, which geographically is like a bridge in the sea to the west, and not because the people from Brittany liked menhirs.

All European mythologies are also directly related to this ritual, as well as mythical stories such as *the Iliad* and *the Odyssey* and the history of *Atlantis*, the classic European tales or other more local tales.

To be reborn, the child-ancestor had to go through three symbolic pregnancies in the womb of his adoptive mother represented by a bear. The belly, the uterus was traditionally a cave, the tomb, in which the child-ancestor fought for nine months (or three times nine months) to go out. During these nine months he was nourished by the placenta, which at the time of his birth became the enemy to fight, the serpent, the dragon, who often seems to want to keep him and could change him into stone like a fetus is actually changed into stone, and an ancestor fossilized if he does not leave the womb or the grave in time. This dragon-serpent with multiple faces must be beheaded as the cord is cut at birth, the child keeping a scar of the "bite" of the latter: the third eye, the navel of knowledge.

The placenta in the uterus nourishes the child with living food, but also and especially here in these ritual pregnancies with knowledge, memory, symbolized and preserved by gold, the only element that has seen everything and who can to record everything (this is why the ring on the finger contains all the life of the individual, the exchange of wedding rings being the exchange of memories, the exchange of lives, symbolized by the gift of *"the door"*: the cervix). This placenta is the last vestige of the ancestor, who gives his last breath to the child to relive in him, the last impulse. The placenta is the father, he is also the one who transforms the mother so that her body accepts the fetus, and is modified to develop and nourish it. In fact, physically, he takes control of the mother's body. It is he who makes pregnancy possible, birth, rebirth, his rebirth.

He is the head of the ancestor, full of knowledge, that the child carries out of the tomb-cave. Thus, the child is represented by a dwarf, a little being (the child) with an old head (the ancestor). The ancestor is then reincarnated, the child is a real individual, he has a name, his name, he has found himself. ***He is reborn.***

Now I have to tell you. For me the wounded man in *the Well* (and thus hidden, concealed, like almost all the man-bird and man-bull chimeras) in *Lascaux*, it is the man who killed his bull opponent. It is the bull-ancestor-spermatozoon caught by the horns and put to death to become placenta-nurturer (hence the entrails coming out). The bird-man is also dead, because it is the image of the ancestor to be reborn. The object at the feet of the man is probably a spear-sling, and the stick-bird is for me a caduceus, a relay, *a perforated baton.*

And now, I said, let me show in a figure how far our nature is enlightened or unenlightened: --Behold! human beings living in a underground den, which has a mouth open towards the light and reaching all along the den; here they have been from their childhood, and have their legs and necks chained so that they cannot move, and can only see before them, being prevented by the chains from turning round their heads. Above and behind them a fire is blazing at a distance, and between the fire and the prisoners there is a raised way; and you will see, if you look, a low wall built along the way, like the screen which marionette players have in front of them, over which they show the puppets.

And do you see, I said, men passing along the wall carrying all sorts of vessels, and statues and figures of animals made of wood and stone and various materials, which appear over the wall? Some of them are talking, others silent.

Like ourselves, I replied; and they see only their own shadows, or the shadows of one another, which the fire throws on the opposite wall of the cave?

And of the objects which are being carried in like manner they would only see the shadows?

And if they were able to converse with one another, would they not suppose that they were naming what was actually before them?

And suppose further that the prison had an echo which came from the other side, would they not be sure to fancy when one of the passers-by spoke that the voice which they heard came from the passing shadow?

To them, I said, the truth would be literally nothing but the shadows of the images.

And now look again, and see what will naturally follow if the prisoners are released and disabused of their error. At first, when any of them is liberated and compelled suddenly to stand up and turn his neck round and walk and look towards the light, he will suffer sharp pains; the glare will distress him, and he will be unable to see the realities of which in his former state he had seen the shadows; and then conceive some one saying to him, that what he saw before was an illusion, but that now, when he is approaching nearer to being and his eye is turned towards more real existence, he has a clearer vision, -what will be his reply? And you may further imagine that his instructor is pointing to the objects as they pass and requiring him to name them, -- will he not be perplexed? Will he not fancy that the shadows which he formerly saw are truer than the objects which are now shown to him?

Plato, *Allegory of the Cave*

Printed in Great Britain
by Amazon